I received a copy of the original version of *Take Another Look at Guidance* in 1972. After reading it, I realized what a special book it was. I went back and read it again, this time underlining key passages, turning down pages, and putting it in my briefcase. Over the years, I found this book a constant companion and a valuable resource. I carried it everyday in my briefcase.

As a business executive, my key role is making decisions and judgments. To do this successfully, it is essential that I receive input or in other words, guidance.

In the world of business we have many sources of guidance . . . computer reports, financial statements, appraisals, trade journals, consultant reports, committee meetings, market research, etc. But for most of us, many times there is something missing.

I am forever grateful to Bob Mumford for writing this book. It has given me that missing decision-making tool: spiritual guidance.

Today, *Take Another Look at Guidance* is still in my briefcase, tattered and worn . . . after 20 years of daily use.

Bob Gorham
Business Executive

TAKE ANOTHER LOOK
AT GUIDANCE

A Study of How God Guides

by

Bob Mumford

PUBLISHED BY
LIFECHANGERS PUBLISHING
RALEIGH, NC

Lifechangers Publishing
P.O. Box 98088
Raleigh, NC 27624
(919) 676-3500

Unless otherwise stated, all Scripture quotations are taken from the *New American Standard Bible*, copyright by The Lockman Foundation, 1960, 1962, 1963, 1968, 1971, 1972, 1973, 1975, 1977.

Verses marked Amplified are taken from the *Amplified New Testament*, copyright by The Lockman Foundation, 1954, 1958.

Verses marked Phillips are taken from the *New Testament in Modern English*, copyright by The Macmillan Company, 1958, 1973.

Fifteenth printing. 210,000 copies in print.

Take Another Look at Guidance has also been translated into: Danish, French, Portuguese, Russian and Spanish.

To the Rev. Walter Beuttler, teacher, spiritual father, friend.
It was he who taught me principles, not methods.

"I cannot do it alone;
    The waves run fast and high,
And the fogs close all around,
    The light goes out in the sky;
But I know that we two
    Shall win in the end,
        Jesus and I.

Coward and wayward and weak,
    I change with the changing sky;
Today so eager and bright,
    Tomorrow too weak to try;
But He never gives in,
    So we two shall win,
        Jesus and I.

I could not guide it myself,
    My boat on life's wild sea;
There's One who sits by my side,
    Who pulls and steers with me.
And I know that we two
    Shall safe enter port,
        Jesus and I."

Streams In The Desert

CONTENTS

PREFACE

There are those who say that God cannot or will not guide us in our day. Others flippantly say, "God led me." The following pages are an attempt to take another look at spiritual guidance in the light of what the Bible teaches on the subject. Neither God nor His Holy Spirit can be reduced to *methods*, but in searching the Scriptural records, we come to recognize that He does work according to clearly outlined *principles*.

This is not a theological treatise or an effort at Biblical scholarship. I simply invite you to take another look with me as we attempt to distinguish God's guidance from the confusion of our own desires, prejudices, preconceived notions, and impulses which clamor for our attention.

We should take great comfort in the promise given us in Isaiah 35:8, "And a highway shall be there, and a way, and it shall be called the Holy Way; the unclean shall not pass over it, but it shall be for the redeemed; the wayfaring men, yes, the simple ones and fools, shall not err in it and lose their way" (Amplified).

My sincere prayer is that *Take Another Look At Guidance* would contribute to your growth, safety, and pleasure along the way. Remember, no man gets lost on a straight road!

Bob Mumford

CHAPTER
1
GUIDANCE . . . FROM WHERE?

Have you ever wondered about your future?

Have you asked yourself: Who am I? Where did I come from? Where am I going?

Have you ever wondered about the purpose of your life?

"Sure," you say, "who hasn't?"

The questions are so basic; it seems almost silly to ask them. But we have all asked them.

So where do you go for your answers?

Ouija Boards and Horoscopes

I read an article one time in Reader's Digest stating that some businessmen, politicians, and prognosticators of our generation read the charts, graphs, and stock-market reports just as some of our forefathers used to read the entrails of chickens.

If you have walked into a bookstore or glanced over the bookracks in the drugstore or supermarket, you have probably noticed how many books deal with one form of guidance or another: How to know your future, how to improve your power of thinking, how to seek the stars for guidance, or how to open your mind to the supernatural wisdom of the universe. The list goes on and on. There are books on interpretation of dreams, on horoscopes, on ESP, mind reading, and how to conduct a seance. There are even books on how to make witches' brew to make yourself irresistible or put a hex on your enemy.

Party games for kids as well as and adults increasingly include Ouija boards, seances, and fortune-telling.

Millions of readers study their daily horoscope in the newspaper "just for fun" or often seriously before deciding on a new job, a new car, or a wedding date. Who has not read or desired to read "prophetess" Jeanne Dixon's predictions or some "New Age" investigation of the future?

How about the batteries of tests given to children in elementary school to determine who he is and what he will be like in the future? Or what about the personality inventories fed into computers to determine what job you are suited for, or what kind of partner you should choose in marriage? These are forms of guidance as well.

Millions of young people try various mind-expanding drugs to "find themselves." Middle-aged couples are stranded in divorce courts. "We made a mistake," they say sadly of ten or twenty years together. "We didn't know ourselves or what we wanted in life."

So life in today's world seems a confused mess with its riots, pollution, wars, and tight economy - and the most we can do is make the best of it.

Or is there a right way, a meaningful purpose for your life, a right vocation, a right partner in marriage? Is there a more predictable way to know who we are and where we are going?

Missing the Mark

Surfers use the expression "right on" to describe a ride on the perfect wave. If you caught the wave just right, it would take you where you wanted to go. The Greeks have a word to describe the exact opposite: *Hamartia.* It means "to miss the mark." All of our strivings to find ourselves and search out our future is with a single purpose in mind. We want to be "right on." We do not want to miss the mark, yet most of us do because we do not know what the mark is. If we do not know where we are going, how can we get there? We are like the man who jumped into the taxi and said, "Take me there!"

The utter confusion among the seekers of truth and guidance in the world stems from the basic fact that they believe all wisdom comes from the same source. The Bible plainly teaches that this is not so. There is wisdom from *above;* that is from God, and there is wisdom from *below;* that is demonic. Both are supernatural. Both can be sought. Both can be found. The Bible also plainly teaches that the wisdom from above is truth. The other is false. One is "right on," leading us to hit the target; the other causes us to "miss the mark."

It is possible to learn to distinguish one from the other. There are obvious and predictable results from following the wisdom from above or the wisdom from below.

The Greek word *hamartia,* to miss the mark, is the word translated in our English Bible as "sin." The Bible teaches that we are born sinners, unable to hit the mark on our own. But the Bible also teaches that God has made several provisions for our condition. He sent Jesus Christ, His only begotten Son, to die on the cross for our missing the mark, thereby reestablishing us in a right relationship with God, our Father. God made the provision, but each individual must accept it for themselves. We are required to exercise our freedom of choice and thereby determine our destiny. We can accept or reject our relationship with God in Christ.

The Secret of Christianity

God's Word tells us that Jesus is the way, the truth, and the life, and that no one can come to the Father any other way. God's Word also says that salvation is the undeserved gift of God, not something earned by our works of goodness. We are saved, not by our own wisdom, cleverness or good deeds, but by repentance and faith in the person and work of Jesus Christ.

We cannot even know what life is all about until we take that first step toward the purposes of God in our own lives. Jesus knows the answer to the age-old riddle of the meaning of life. He declared that He knew from whence He came, who He was, and where He was going (John 8:14). It is He who desires to bring the same certainty to us.

The Apostle Paul tells us that the secret of Christianity is that Christ actually dwells in the believer by faith. With Jesus Christ in us, we can begin to focus on what life is all about for us personally.

Now God has made another provision for our guidance. John the Baptist, who baptized in water those who repented of their sins and turned from their wrong doings, said of Jesus Christ that He would baptize the believer in the Holy Spirit. In the book of Acts we read again and again that this was the common experience for the new converts to Christianity.

Peter tells the people of Israel gathered at Jerusalem for the celebration of Pentecost: "Repent, and let each of you be baptized in the name of Jesus Christ for the forgiveness of your sins; and you shall receive the gift of the Holy Spirit" (Acts 2:38).

Jesus talks about the Holy Spirit in John 16:13, "But when He, the Spirit of truth, comes, He will guide you into all the truth; for He will not speak on His own initiative, but whatever He hears, He will speak; and He will disclose to you what is to come."

The Holy Spirit is a gift, a promise, and here again, we are faced with a choice: To ask and receive it or reject it. Again our destiny will be effected by our decision. It is a question of surrendering our will and our opinion to the will of God as revealed in the Scriptures.

Jesus came into our lives through salvation, and we were born again of the Spirit. So He is our Savior, but how much of us does He have? An encounter with the person of the Holy Spirit takes us another step into God's will for us. We surrender more of our being to Him.

Another provision God has made available for our guidance is His Word, the Bible. Without Scriptures, it is impossible to hit the mark in our lives. It is impossible for us to know the will and purposes of God. These must be revealed to us.

Jesus told the Jews who believed on Him, "If you abide in My word, then you are truly disciples of Mine; and you

shall know the truth, and the truth shall make you free"
(John 8:31-32).

Again we are faced with a choice: to accept the Word of
God as truth or refuse it. Again our choice will effect our
destiny of whether or not we will hit the target and move on
into God's will and purpose for our lives.

We all live by some authority, whether Pluto or Plato.
Jesus said, "Blessed is the man who makes God's Word to be
his authority for he will never be disappointed or put to
shame!"(I Peter 2:6).

Two Sources of Wisdom

Now let us assume that you have taken the first steps
outlined for us by the Word of God. You have confessed and
repented of your sins, accepted Jesus' death on the cross in
your stead, and received the promises and the Baptism in the
Holy Spirit. You have decided to read the Bible more and
to accept it as truth.

Surely now you have tuned in on the wisdom from above
and have begun to tune out the confusing impulses from
any other source. Unfortunately, it is not quite that simple.

Much of the confusion about guidance among Christians comes from the sad fact that we do not recognize that
we are exposed to counterfeit "wisdom" which is not from
God. Satan deals with both nonbelievers and believers, but
he deals with each differently. John Wesley's instructions
were that we should not hastily ascribe things to God. Do
not easily suppose dreams, voices, impressions, visions, or
revelations to be from God. They may be from Him; they
may be Satanic. "Beloved, do not believe every spirit, but

test the spirits to see whether they are from God" (I John 4:1).

The Bible promises that a serious child of God can know the perfect will of God for his life and experience the joy, reality, and fullness of divine guidance. We do not want to overemphasize the danger of negative or false guidance, but it is important to sound a warning at the start in order to determine what guidance is NOT.

Familiar Spirits

Once a young man at a college where I taught came to me and said, "Bob, I have a wonderful form of guidance. There is a presence surrounding me. Anytime I ask a question, I receive an immediate answer from this presence."

Immediately I became suspicious and questioned the young man. It was apparent that he was involved with what the Bible calls a "familiar spirit." Having a "familiar spirit" simply means he had cultivated a relationship and became familiar with a spirit from the supernatural world below. This spirit, as is often the case, was posing as the Holy Spirit, but the young man could not tell the difference.

I weighed this matter in my heart and asked God for discernment. Two days later the young man was in my office again, and I asked him point-blank, "Have you ever been involved with witchcraft or fortune-telling?"

His eyes took on a strange look as though they could see right through me, and he said, "How did you know? When I was a child, my mother used to take me to fortune-tellers."

Asking him to sit down, I opened my Bible and read: "There shall not be found among you anyone who makes his son or his daughter pass through the fire, one who uses divination, one who practices witchcraft, or one who interprets omens, or a sorcerer, or one who casts a spell, or a medium, or a spiritist, or one who calls up the dead. For whoever does these things is detestable to the Lord; and because of these detestable things the Lord your God will drive them out before you. You shall be blameless before the Lord your God" (Deut. 18:10-13).

Then I explained: "Divination means fortune-telling. An observer of the times is an astrologer. An enchanter is a genuine magician, performing not childish parlor tricks but actual works of magic. A witch is a sorcerer. A charmer is a hypnotist. A consulter with familiar spirits is a medium with a 'guide.' A wizard is a clairvoyant or psychic. A necromancer is one who consults with the dead."

As I talked, the presence of the Holy Spirit became apparent in the room and a look of understanding dawned in the young man's eyes. "People use these counterfeit means of guidance to unveil hidden knowledge, ascertain future events, uncover secret wisdom, and exercise super-natural power," I said. "But you see, all this and more can be found through the Holy Spirit. Are you willing to surrender this counterfeit form of guidance for one that is genuine and Biblical?"

He nodded and said he wanted true deliverance. We prayed for release according to the new covenant which was provided in the blood of Jesus Christ. He stepped out of my office a new man.

The demonic realm has a very special arsenal of weapons which they use against the Christian. They seek to get to us through superheated impulses and uncontrolled imaginations. Satan seduces, deceives, accuses, and condemns. He is the master of false guidance and deception.

The key word here is, of course, deception. Satan is a liar. It is imperative for us to acquaint ourselves thoroughly with the truth of God's Word which is the antidote to lies and deceptions. Thus, through the ministry of the Holy Spirit, we will recognize a lie when we are required to judge. This is the armor God has provided so that we can withstand every fiery dart from Satan.

God Told Me to Do It

It is tragic that many misled, misinformed people have committed indescribable acts of horror and immorality and later, when questioned by the proper authority, they have said, "God spoke to me and told me to do it." They may have heard a voice, but had they known God as He reveals Himself through His Word, His Spirit, and His Son, they would never have received the false guidance let alone acted on it.

A Skill to Be Learned

Divine guidance is further complicated by the trickery of our own mixed-up emotions, our impure motives, our prejudices, and old habit patterns of thought and action. It is at this point that some who have seen the obstacles or know of some particular or spectacular failure turn their backs in fear or become prejudice against a deeper commitment to God's way. Many churches have clamped the lid on the possibility that God could speak to His children today. Assuming a defensive position, they declare that because He has already "spoken through His Son" in the Scriptures, present guidance is unneeded or superfluous. Their accepted interpretation of Hebrews 1:2 seems to suggest that direct guidance by the Holy Spirit was strictly for the Church of the first century. They say, "We are living in a different era and do not need supernatural, divine guidance that comes through the gifts and manifestations of the Holy Spirit."

On the other hand there are those who boast of deep mystical experiences in the realm of the Spirit and who look down their noses at those unaware of the "deeper mysteries." I would like to suggest that both groups are in danger of missing the mark. While these people seem to look at the world as either natural or supernatural, the reality is that our lives should be a *balance of both*.

Careful Failures

The man who chooses to live entirely in the natural thinks he is safe. He says, "By rejecting the mystical and keeping myself solidly based on the Word of God, I will never go astray." Perhaps this holds some truth. But he will never enjoy that intimate walk with God, guided by the presence of the Holy Spirit, that the Scriptures suggest is part of the normal Christian experience. He may be safe, but he will be robbed of the delights that are the rewards of a more adventurous soul. He may be classified as *the careful failure*.

The twelve disciples were together in a boat at sea when Jesus came walking toward them on the water. Peter cried out, "Lord, if it is You, command me to come to You on the water" (Matt. 14:28). Jesus said, "Come!" So, Peter got out of the boat and walked on water. Yes, he did start to sink and it was a fearful experience. But consider the eleven *careful failures* who remained in the boat. They did not even *attempt* to walk on the water.

Peter, whose heart cried out for all that God had for him, took the risk. He made that leap of faith into a state of trusting God. Peter, the adventurous, impulsive one who sometimes made eager promises he could not keep, later became the rock, the obedient, solid one.

If you have honestly set your goal to be led of the Spirit, then you must learn four basic principles about guidance.

First, guidance does not come automatically. You cannot push a button, open your Bible at random looking for a verse or listen for voices.

Second, receiving guidance is a skill to be learned, often through trial and error, which will demand some spiritual adventure on your part. False starts and wrong assumptions do form part of the lessons.

Third, receiving guidance is not a set of methods, but is based on obedience to a set of principles.

Fourth, guidance is intensely personal. It is a relationship between you and your Father God through Jesus Christ and the person of the Holy Spirit. It is God's guidance for your life and only you can receive it from Him (Eph. 2:18).

A final word of caution: A decision to earnestly seek God's guidance and plan for our lives necessitates a clean break with all other forms of guidance. The Bible lists all attempts at seeking to know the future by any means other than the direct revelation of God as sin and therefore something we must confess, repent of, and turn from. This specifically includes all forms of spiritism, seances, fortune-telling, card-reading, crystal-ball gazing, channelling, astrology, horoscopes, Ouija boards, palm reading, handwriting analysis, ESP, clairvoyance, mind reading, parapsychology, science of mind religions, and other related methods.

There can be absolutely no compromise in this realm for the Christian, because this is precisely how the supernatural wisdom from below, Satan's counterfeit, gains access to our lives. The consequences have been tragic for those who have opened themselves to these influences: agony, despair, mental torment, confusion, depression, and for some, suicide.

In James we find a clear description of the two forms of supernatural wisdom: "This wisdom is not that which comes down from above, but is earthly, natural, demonic" (Jam. 3:15). Other translations give you these words: "There is a wisdom that is a supernatural wisdom which does not come from above." It is a supernatural power which works in the same way as divine guidance. A literal translation describing the fruit of this wisdom goes like this: "But where there is a supernatural wisdom working which is not from above, but is really earthly and natural, that is, soulish and inspired by demons, there is jealousy, rivalry, tumult, and every worthless practice."

In direct contrast is James' description of the wisdom which comes from above: "But the wisdom (the guidance, the leading of the Spirit of God) from above is first pure, then peaceable, gentle, reasonable (teachable, not rigid), full of mercy and good fruits, unwavering, without hypocrisy. And the seed whose fruit is righteousness is sown in peace by them who make peace" (Jam. 3:17-18). The Amplified Bible says: "But the wisdom from above is first of all pure (undefiled); then it is peace-loving, courteous (considerate, gentle). [It is willing to] yield to reason, full of compassion and good fruits; it is wholehearted and straightforward, impartial and unfeigned - free from doubts, wavering and insincerity. And the harvest of righteousness (of conformity to God's will in thought and deed) is [the fruit of the seed] sown in peace by those who work for and make peace - in themselves and in others, [that is] that peace which means concord (agreement, harmony) between individuals, with undisturbedness, in a peaceful mind free from fears and agitating passions and moral conflicts."

Certain Guidance

As we begin to seek God's guidance for our lives, we must be willing to submit the *impressions* we receive to the examination and evaluation of Biblical principle. God's Word is the final judge and that means it must take precedence over our emotions, feelings, impressions, any signs, or leadings we have received. God's Word must take precedence over our subjective confidence that God has indeed spoken to us in some personal revelation.

If some form of spiritual guidance does not agree with God's Word and pass the test of James 3, our source of wisdom must be assessed as not originating from above and must consequently be refused, however convinced we are that it is "of God"!

A note of reassurance: As we grow in maturity, both in the Word and in the knowledge of our Lord and Savior Jesus Christ, we can learn to be as sure about our guidance as we are about our salvation. We *can* know the fruits of guidance and recognize that we are not being deceived. We *can* distinguish between the guidance of the Holy Spirit and the subtle counterfeit of Satan. We *can*, as well, avoid being led down dead-end streets, fruitless activities, or subjective confusion.

Romans 8:14 says, "For all who are being led by the Spirit of God, these are the sons of God.". When you allow yourself to be disciplined and trained to the leading of God's Holy Spirit, you are then showing the quality of a mature son.

CHAPTER
2
MY WAY -- OR GOD'S WAY?

The danger in using familiar words is that we sometimes lose site of their meaning. Many Christians talk loosely about the "saved" and the "sinners." "Saved" usually denotes the ones who have accepted Jesus and are on their way to heaven. "Sinners" categorizes the rest of mankind, those who have rejected Jesus Christ and consequently are condemned. This is such a dangerous oversimplification that it leads to error.

The Bull's Eye

True acceptance or rejection of Jesus Christ as the Redeemer who died on the cross for our sins is the key to salvation and eternal life. It must be remembered, however, that "sin" is a translation of the Greek word *hamartia*, meaning to "miss the mark." Thus if we imply that all those who have accepted Christ and are born of the Spirit have automatically hit the bull's-eye and are now fulfilling God's highest purpose and plan for their lives, then we need to redefine our terminology. Acceptance of Jesus Christ as the Redeemer for one's personal life is the basic requirement for those who desire to know God, but it is very possible to be a believer in Jesus Christ and still miss God's purpose and plan for your life.

Father's Pleasure

A father, on his way home from work, decided to take his little son downtown for a treat at the ice cream parlor. When he got home, he found his son in the backyard playing in the mud. The father did not change his mind about the ice cream parlor though. He brought the little boy inside, gave him a bath, put clean clothes on him and said, "Son, now we're going to the ice cream parlor for a treat."

The little boy, being a true fundamentalist, said, "Daddy, I don't want to go. I want to stay here by the bathtub and tell everybody how dirty I was and how good you've been to me."

"But you don't understand why I cleaned you up," the father said. "I want you to go with me." The son almost missed the father's intended purpose. We need to be careful we do not miss the mark.

Hitting the Mark

In II Timothy 1:9 we read, "Who has saved us, and called us with a holy calling, not according to our works, but according to His own purpose and grace. . . ." Jesus found us in the mud, cleaned us up, and redeemed us from sin by His death on the cross in order that we *could* live for Him. Yet many a Christian gives thanks to God for the salvation of his soul but continues *living* his life in the same old way. Such Christians follow their own desires and ideas, their own guidance, and initiative.

God's purpose, simply stated, was to save us *from sin unto* His eternal purpose. We literally owe Him our lives and one day we will be held accountable for what we have done with every hour, action, word and thought. Hitting the mark means that we live our lives so totally yielded to God that His will becomes our guide and that every moment of our lives are lived in perfect accord with His plan and purpose for us. If this is so, then some who are simply saved by faith in Jesus Christ have missed the mark so far that it is pathetic. Correcting this is one of our purposes in this book.

The God of Justice

How does God deal with us, His children, when we deliberately go our own way? Does He deal with us at all or are we free to choose our own way of life once we have entered the door of our salvation experience? If salvation is a free gift, why would there be any strings attached?

We are living in times of great permissiveness in child rearing, in school discipline (or lack of it), and in rebellion against all kinds of authority whether it be parental, police, or papal. The courts where the "rights" of criminals are often considered before the rights of the innocent victims of crime, just add to this national attitude. Even in our churches we are being taught situational ethics where morality is a flexible thing, not conforming to any set standard (such as that determined by the Bible). Perhaps it is time to have a lesson in justice from God, who is Justice.

In the second chapter of Jeremiah we find the prophet sent by God to warn His people who had willfully missed the mark by going astray. At one time they had walked with God. He had brought them out of Egypt and saved them from bondage. They had known His commandments, and

He had made a covenant with them to bless them and make them a blessing to others. But they had persisted in *going their own way.* Through the words of the prophet, God reminded His people that they once loved Him and He had protected them from evil. But then He asks, "What injustice did your fathers find in Me, that they went far from Me and walked after emptiness and became empty? And they did not say, 'Where is the Lord . . . ?'" (Jer. 2:5-6).

There are Christians today in the same condition. God saved them from bondage and led them out of their personal Egypt, but now they go their own way; they are unaware of the absence or the presence of the Lord, for they have forgotten Him.

I believe there are churches today that have become such organized marvels of religious activity, so propped up by human programs and initiatives that they would not miss God for a moment if He left. They are running a business and therefore are not dependent on the supernatural manifestations of God. Like the children of Judah, no one among them is asking, "Where is the Lord?"

Cistern or Well

God describes what His people have done. "For My people have committed two evils: They have forsaken Me, the fountain of living waters, to hew for themselves cisterns, broken cisterns, that can hold no water" (Jer. 2:13). There is a fundamental difference between a fresh flowing well and a cistern. A cistern is hewed out of solid stone or in modern times made from concrete. Its purpose is simply to hold water that has been poured into it - water, yes, but stale and warm. In contrast, when a well is dug, it is lined with rocks and water flows through it. At first a well does not give much water, and that is why we are told to keep pumping a new well. The more we pump, the more the water flows through, because the veins carrying the water begin to clear. We have tapped an underground stream that is ever fresh and never runs dry.

The Christian who has *forsaken* the Well of Living Water has missed the mark. Instead he has hewed out for himself a container for storing stale religious activity and doctrines. Instead of being a daily walk with a living Jesus, his Christianity becomes a "canned affair." Have you ever heard a sermon from a cistern? Unfortunately, there are some in almost every pastor's notebook. And the idea of a preacher reaching into his "barrel" (cistern) to find the message of the morning is more frightening than funny.

God's Cure

The people of Judah turned their backs on God while He was leading them in the way. This is serious business, and some of us are guilty of it even today. Now what are the consequences? Some who are rebelling against God expect Him to come after them to coax and coerce, but look at Jeremiah 2:19, "'Your own wickedness will correct you, and your apostasies will reprove you; know therefore and see that it is evil and bitter for you to forsake the Lord your God, and the dread of Me is not in you,' declares the Lord God of hosts." When you insist on your own way, God's *cure* may be an overabundant supply of what you are asking for until you wish you never had it.

A young lady who was a student in the Bible college where I taught said, "Oh, God, *I must* have that young man, I just must." God's guidance was repeatedly negative, but she kept insisting, until the restraint was lifted and God acquiesced regarding their marriage. About a year and a half later, while she was still in Bible college, her husband developed a severe drinking problem. The principle of Jeremiah 2:19 was brought into effect as she was required to help him up the stairs nearly every night.

If you insist on your own way -- you're going to get it!

Later in the same chapter of Jeremiah we find another picture of the consequences of our rebellion: "A wild donkey accustomed to the wilderness, that sniffs the wind in her passion. In the time of her heat who can turn her away?" (Jer. 2:24). The prophet pictures human nature as a wild ass -- a young donkey, self-willed and stubborn, seeking her own satisfaction and pleasure.

Have you ever been in that condition? You set your course, unyielding to reason or persuasion saying, "This is what I'm going to do, and I could care less how it affects the will of God or anybody else!"

The last part of the verse says, "All who seek her will not become weary; *in her month they will find her.*" What is God saying? He is saying that while we are still running, He will not send anybody to run after us. He knows that the rebellion we carry inside will bear fruit; we will be pregnant with the consequences. In due time, while we are in labor with our full-term troubles, He will find us and speak to us again. Hopefully, we will be ready to listen and open to guidance. The children of Judah were not. In Jeremiah 2:30

God cries through His prophet, "In vain I have struck your sons; they have accepted no chastening. Your sword has devoured your prophets like a destroying lion."

I know there are some people who wish that verse was not in the Bible. "God would never do a thing like that," they say. But God will do what He says He will do in order to get us to listen. We ought to realize this and not deceive ourselves or blame all our misfortune on bad luck, the devil, or the national economy. *Maybe God is talking to us.*

Guide of My Youth

But what did the children of Judah do? Their reaction is recorded in Jeremiah 2:31, "Why do My people say, 'We are free to roam; we will come no more to Thee?'" These are God's own people speaking. "But they said, 'We will not walk in it.' And I set watchmen over you, saying, 'Listen to the sound of the trumpet!' But they said, 'We will not listen'" (Jer. 6:16,17). Essentially they are saying, "We have dominion over ourselves; we will never submit to You or Your demands on our lives. We enjoy our illegal liberty."

They are talking like a teenager who thought his parents were too strict. Finally reaching the omniscient age of eighteen (or maybe today it is thirteen), he kicks off all the braces and says to his father, "I will never come under your roof again; I am my own boss now." What can Dad say? He knows what must happen, and he will be around to help pick up the pieces, but his father's-heart wishes that he could prevent his son from hurting himself.

The children of Judah did not really believe that calamity would fall on them. They said confidently, "Because I am innocent, surely His anger shall turn from me" (Jer. 2:35). They were wrong. In Jeremiah 2:37 the prophet said, "From this place also you shall go out with your hands on your head; for the Lord has rejected those in whom you trust, and you shall not prosper with them." And it literally came to pass. With their hands upon their heads they were led into captivity to Babylon. They wanted to enjoy their freedom -- but became slaves instead.

Yet, even then, God continued to plead with them through His prophet. In Jeremiah 3:4 He said, "Have you not just now called to Me, 'My Father, Thou art the friend of my youth?'" What were all the teachings and dealings designed to do in their lives? *God wanted them to want Him.* "My Father, will You guide me even from my youth?"

Guidance is something we must embrace, ask for, and desire. Why are most people afraid of submitting to God's guidance?

Imagine your sixteen-year-old son. He has been getting a little wild lately, wanting some wheels, more liberty, more money. Then one day he says, "Dad, may I talk to you?"

"Sure!" You have been wanting to have a few words with him yourself.

"Dad, I have been thinking a lot lately. You know I used to think I knew everything about life and what I was going to do, but I am beginning to realize that I am still just a kid. You have been around a lot longer than me, Dad, and I am beginning to understand that you really want what is best for me. Dad, from now on I want you to guide and direct me and show me the right way to go. Whatever you say, I will try to obey."

Would you say to your son, "I want you to go to your room and be restricted for six months"? Some people think that if they ever really submitted to God, He would ask them to do something they could not or did not want to do. But God never demands the unjust or the impossible. He wants our submission and in response He promises to tenderly guide us.

Have you ever gone your own way -- and been sorry you did? Have you ever been glad you went God's way, even if you did not like it at first?

That is the way it works!

There is a song we often sing in church; most of us think of it as an appeal to the unsaved, but it is really a song of submission -- the consecration of a son to his Father:

I've wandered far away from God,
Now I'm coming home.
The paths of sin too long I've trod,
Lord, I'm coming home.

Chorus:
Coming home, coming home,
Never more to roam,
Open wide Thine arms of love,
Lord, I'm coming home.
(*Coming Home,* Redemption Hymnal)

To wander does not mean you are not a son; it does mean that in your rebellion and self-will you have not submitted to the counsel of your Father.

We know the rebellion of our human hearts. We want to hit the mark, but when God begins to lead us, we find it difficult to follow. If we are young, we say, "But, I want to live my own life." If we are married, in business, or caught in peculiar circumstances, we say, "But God, You just do not understand. In some parts of my life I have got to have my own way; Your way is just too narrow, strict, and religious."

God *does* understand. He knows the beginning *and* the end. He loves us with an eternal love and is working in our lives to bring us to the place where He can daily lead us -- in our finances, in our relationships with others, in our physical needs, in our spiritual walk.

As you ask for and submit to guidance, you will find God taking the *initiative* in your life, adjusting and rear-ranging where you have been off the track. If you say, "Yes, Lord," to Him, you will find Him leading you in a new way. And, by the way, you will never find His demands greater than what you can produce. Philippians 2:13 promises us: "For it is God who is at work in you, both to will and to work for His good pleasure." Later in the same letter Paul writes, "I am ready for anything through the strength of the one who lives within me" (Phil. 4:13 Phillips).

God is *not* guilty of being willing to guide some and not others. We shut ourselves off from genuine guidance by following our own desires and coating them with a veneer of pretended obedience. Human desires are masked as guidance in order to make rebellion palatable to ourselves and others. The result is self-deception and a rejection of true guidance. The monumental illustration of this is Saul, the king of Israel, who in self-will refused to obey, causing

Samuel to declare, "For rebellion is as the sin of witchcraft, and stubbornness is as idolatry and teraphim (good luck images). Because you have rejected the word of the Lord, He also has rejected you from being king" (I Sam. 15:23 Amplified).

Divine guidance is for all of God's children who *ask* to be guided, *submit* to Him who is the Guide, and refuse to follow their own human desires.

CHAPTER
3
LUCK . . . OR HAPPENSTANCE?

When we, like errant sons and daughters, return to our father and say, "Father, I *want* You to be the guide of my youth," something begins to happen. God begins to guide our lives in a new way. He then begins to take a particular kind of initiative toward us. We misunderstand greatly, however, if we believe this is always going to happen in some spectacular way.

God's Providence

When we talk about divine guidance, most people think in terms of dreams, visions, prophecies, angels, and voices. These all have a place in divine guidance. *However, most guidance occurs when we are not even conscious of it.* God knows the beginning and the end. He arranges circumstances. Sometimes we are required to take another look at where we have been in order to recognize if God has been guiding us at all!

When we take a closer look at the cases of obvious guidance in the Bible -- and in our own lives -- we may discover that direct intervention from God is usually for the purpose of adjusting or correcting the way of His children, much as a space scientist would make an in-flight course correction on a rocket speeding toward the moon. This may come as a blow to our spiritual pride, for we would like to say, "I am becoming spiritual; God led me this evening. He allowed me to have a flat tire on the way to the airport. I missed my flight, and the plane crashed on takeoff killing everyone on board." This is not to say God does not sometimes work sensationally, but usually God's guidance is so natural that the Spirit-led Christian might not even be aware of it.

God's providence works on a narrow, dangerous margin. This, I believe, is a fundamental principle in divine guidance. Sometimes God is required to interfere directly in our lives to prevent us from messing up the plan He has for us. An accident, a phone call, a chance meeting, or a perfectly timed letter causes us to look back and say, "That was God's timing! He knew the beginning and the end. He led me even when I did not know it."

This form of guidance is what we will term *unconscious guidance* and it begins when we meet several conditions -- the first being that we must place ourselves in a childlike relationship to God and submit to His will for our life. Often, in the eternal council of God, unconscious guidance has operated before we ever made the discovery that God was actually guiding us.

Sincerity and Guidance

The initial commitment to God is something like getting on a train. Once you are on board you do not worry about the intersections or the red and green lights. They are the engineer's job. *Your* responsibility is to get on the right train.

Once I was having lunch in a Philadelphia restaurant and got into a conversation with a waitress who was not a believer in Jesus Christ. She said, "Well, I feel like I am sincere and that is what counts, isn't it? As long as you are sincere it does not really matter what you believe. We are all going to the same place in the end."

I thought, *Dear Lord, what am I going to say to this lady?* Then I remembered about the train. "What if you want to go to Miami," I said, "and you get on a train bound for New York City? You sit there and say, 'I believe I'm going to Miami.' And you are very sincere about it. Now when that train pulls into Grand Central Station, where do you think you will be, in New York or Miami?"

"Oh," she said, "I understand." I hope she did, because *sincerity is not guidance.*

Christian Luck

How then does this "unconscious" form of guidance work? Let's look at a couple of examples in the Bible. The first one is in the book of Ruth.

Naomi was a widow and she was returning to her native Israel. Her daughter-in-law, Ruth, was a gentile. Naomi said, "Ruth, you must stay here in your own land, find yourself a husband and live happily with him." But Ruth refused to stay. She clung to Naomi and said, "Do not urge me to leave you or turn back from following you; for where you go, I will go, and where you lodge, I will lodge. Your people shall be my people, and your God, my God" (Ruth 1:16). Ruth committed herself to Naomi and to God. Ruth wanted to serve Naomi and her God forever, even until

death. She said, "Where you die, I will die, and there I will
be buried. Thus may the Lord do to me, and worse, if
anything but death parts you and me" (Ruth 1:17).

Now this is unreserved commitment to God, a presup-
position for guidance, and the lack of it is the cause of many
problems in divine guidance.

So Naomi and Ruth went back to Bethlehem, Naomi's
hometown. But outwardly they did not see the immediate
fulfillment of God's promised blessing. Things were rough
for them. They were poor, and one day the poverty caused
Ruth to go out and find some grain to make their bread.
This was during the barley harvest and the poor were
allowed to come into the fields after the reapers had gathered
the grain and glean what the reapers had overlooked.
Things were so bad she had to live as a scavenger. There was
still no outward evidence of God's guidance and concern.

Now notice an interesting verse: "So she departed and
went and gleaned in the field after the reapers; and she
happened to come to the portion of the field belonging to
Boaz, who was of the family of Elimelech" (Ruth 2:3).
Elimelech was Naomi's husband who had died.

God's response to that kind of commitment is found in
Ruth 2:12: "May the Lord reward your work, and your
wages be full from the Lord, the God of Israel, under whose
wings you have come to seek refuge." Ruth had put herself
into God's hands and He promised to keep her.

How did Ruth get her guidance so that she *just happened*
to glean in Boaz's field? Did she say, "Oh, God, speak to me
in a vision and tell me what field to glean in?" No, Ruth was
simply doing her duty, working her way patiently between

the rows, picking up the few grains she could find and she just happened to wind up in Boaz's field.

The world calls it *luck*. The Christian calls it *providence!* But as Ruth was concentrating on doing her duty, her "hap" happened. She was in the right field, at the right time, doing the right thing, to meet the right man. And so, because of her unreserved commitment to God and her willingness to do menial tasks, even when she did not see God's providence at work, He arranged the circumstances. Ruth married Boaz, and they had a son who became David's grandfather. Ruth is one of the few gentiles in the lineage of Jesus Christ, and it is thrilling to think of how she just happened to be in that position.

Consider how many times you just happen to be in the right place at the right time!

Commitment

A minister friend told me the story of driving across Florida with his family. When his wife said, "Let's stop and get some orange juice for the children," he agreed and they just happened to turn off at a certain exit, drove down a block or two, and happened to pull up in front of a certain fruit-stand. Before he had time to get out of the car, a lady came running across the street, directly up to his car.

"Are you a minister?" she asked breathlessly.

"Yes," he replied.

"Thank God!" she exclaimed. "This morning I prayed that God would send a minister who would lay hands on me and pray for my healing. God said you would be driving a station wagon and be pulling a trailer." She looked at the evangelist's brown station wagon and trailer and asked, "What took you so long?"

The minister and his wife did not know anything about God's plan for them that afternoon. They had not heard a voice say, "Turn off at this exit and drive two blocks to the fruit-stand where there is a lady I want you to pray for." But they *had* committed that day to God and prayed before leaving that His will and plan for that day would come to pass. When we do this, we begin to find ourselves in the right place at the right time for God's providence to work in our behalf. It is adventurous!

Beginning in the Way

Let's look at some other conditions for perfect "unconscious" guidance. The story of Abraham's servant, who was sent to find a wife for Isaac, is a classic example of guidance. If we look at the entire story in Genesis 24, we find at least *three* specific presuppositions for this kind of perfect unconscious guidance.

In verses 3 and 4, Abraham had said to his oldest and most trusted servant: "And I will make you swear by the Lord, the God of heaven and the God of earth, that you shall not take a wife for my son from the daughters of the Canaanites, among whom I live, but you shall go to my country and to my relatives, and take a wife for my son Isaac."

The *first* premise: The servant was made to promise to maintain a separation from the world. Abraham wanted Isaac to be holy and undefiled in the presence of the Lord.

This is the first condition in qualifying for God's "unconscious guidance" in our lives.

Now look at verse 7, "The Lord, the God of heaven, who took me from my father's house and from the land of my birth, and who spoke to me, and who swore to me, saying, 'To your descendants I will give this land,' He will send His angel before you, and you will take a wife for my son from there."

The *second* premise: They believed the word of God. Abraham said, "Listen, God promised to find my son a wife and I believe Him." This trust was a fundamental aspect of Abraham's relationship with God and a second vital condition in our being open to God's guidance.

The servant then obtained ten camels and started on his way saying, "O Lord, the God of my master Abraham, please grant me success today, and show lovingkindness to my master Abraham" (vs. 12).

The *third* premise: The entire journey (or mission) was soaked in prayer. I don't mean just prayer for specifics, I mean soaked, steeped in prayer. The servant's soul was poised toward God -- a final condition we must practice in our lives if we are to be in a position to appropriate God's guidance.

The servant came to the well outside the city at evening time, knowing the women would come out to draw water. He continued talking to God in prayer: "Behold, I am standing by the spring, and the daughters of the men of the city are coming out to draw water; now may it be that the girl to whom I say, 'Please let down your jar so that I may drink,' and who answers, 'Drink, and I will water your camels also'; - may she be the one whom Thou hast appointed for Thy servant Isaac; and by this I shall know that Thou hast shown lovingkindness to my master" (Gen. 24:13-14).

What happened? Read verse 15, "And it came about before he had finished speaking, that behold, Rebekah came out. . . ." Do you think God had whispered in Rebekah's ear, "Rebekah, I want you to go to the well; there is a man up there . . .?" No, Rebekah, just like Ruth, came to the well because it was time to draw water. It was her duty to be there.

Had God whispered in the servant's ear, "Go to that well; I will send a girl"? No, the servant went to the well because he was tired, sweaty and thirsty after a long day's travel. He stood there, not knowing what to do next. It was in desperation that he said, "I am going to trust You, Lord. The first girl I speak to who volunteers to draw water for me and my camels will be the one, Lord."

And when Rebekah gave the servant a drink from her pitcher and volunteered to draw water for his camels, the servant bowed his head and worshipped God: "Oh, Lord, I thank You. I didn't know where to find a bride for Isaac, but You led me over many miles, and I just happened to come to the right well at the right time to meet the right woman."

First, there is a commitment which involves a separation unto God. Second, a trusting in His word, His promises. And finally, a life steeped in prayer, and a soul poised toward God.

That is getting on the right train. The rest is up to the engineer and conductor.

God's Conductor

So far we have been dealing with unconscious, providential guidance. But if during your journey it becomes necessary to change trains, who is responsible for letting us know when to get off and which one to take next? The conductor, of course. If God the Father is the Engineer, then the Conductor must be the Holy Spirit.

To change trains we need *special guidance.* That is when the Conductor comes along with a dream, a vision, a prophetic word, a miracle, or some other kind of specific direction.

So we are talking about two forms of guidance -- *unconscious, providential guidance* because our lives are committed to Jesus Christ and *special guidance* when God wants to move us into a new direction, a new job, or a new field.

An example of this is found in Luke 2:27 and again in Luke 2:38. Simeon had received a special revelation from the Holy Spirit that he should go to the Temple. He arrived just at the time the parents of Jesus brought the child for circumcision. However, old Anna received no such special revelation. She was just going to the Temple to fast and pray and she just "happened" to arrive at the time the Christ child appeared. But both Simeon and Anna were there by divine timing.

Perhaps you have said, "Well, if I could hear a voice I would be at the right place at the right time, too." But look at Anna who just happened to be there. Like Ruth and Rebekah *she was just doing her duty* and God blessed her in the process.

We need to learn to relieve the strain of feeling that since we may have difficulty in hearing God's voice, we cannot be guided. God leads one by voices and another by circumstances. But He leads both to Christ. Once we have made our commitment to the Lord, we can *expect* to be in the right field, by the right well, in the right temple, or on the right street at the right time.

CHAPTER
4
KNOWING THE WILL OF GOD!

Majoring in Minors

As Christians, we too often major in minors. We pray, "Oh, Lord help us pay the rent." "Help me find a new job." "I need a new car, Lord." Those should be our minor concerns.

Paul approached things differently. He had a specific request for the brand new church at Colossae, "We have not ceased to pray for you and to ask that you may be *filled with the knowledge of His will* in all spiritual wisdom and understanding" (Col. 1:9). This is majoring in majors. The basic and underlying premise for all divine guidance is that it is possible to know the will of God! This should be at the top of our prayer list for ourselves and others.

God originally created man that He might have communion with him. Man was created with the ability to know God. But man's rebellion and sin (his inability to "hit the mark") broke the lines of communication. Through Christ we have been given the opportunity to restore that intimate fellowship with God, and this is the goal which we are seeking. *Learning the skill of receiving divine guidance is learning to walk in intimate fellowship with God.* The problem at the outset is that our minds and our intellects are quite out of tune with God and blinded by the sin within and around us.

Seven Expected Results

When my children were little I often laid my hands on them at night and prayed, "Oh, God, give them a capacity to know You." Now all four of my children and their spouses are walking with the Lord in a meaningful relationship with Him. I knew that if they could only come to know God, everything else in their lives would fall into place. Jesus said it too, "But seek first His kingdom and His righteousness; and all these things shall be added to you" (Matt. 6:33).

Paul had observed what happened in a man's life when he came to know the will of God. In his letter to the Colossians he lists eight expected results: "So that you may *walk in a manner worthy* of the Lord, *to please Him in all respects, bearing fruit* in every good work and *increasing in the knowledge of God; strengthened* with all power, according to His glorious might, for the attaining of all *steadfastness and patience;* joyously giving thanks to the Father, who has qualified us to *share in the inheritance* of the saints in light" (Col. 1:10-12). In order to *walk worthy* of the Lord, we must know what He wants from us. Jesus was a Father-pleaser. He walked in a manner that was pleasing to His Father in all respects.

Father-Pleasers

God once impressed on me the need to focus in on a single goal for my life. As I did so, one by one my prayer requests were reduced to a specific prayer: "Father, I want to be a son who can please You." I began to realize God wanted me to major in majors.

Most men are *self-pleasers*. Others are *man-pleasers*. But until men reach the stage of wanting to be *God-pleasers* they will never be able to fully understand the will of the Father for their lives. It is only by doing the will of God that our lives become fruitful. Perhaps you have met people who have been Christians for years, yet never led another person to Christ. They complain, "What's the matter with me? Maybe I should read a book on how to win souls and influence people!" They don't need to read a book; they need to be in the will of God.

Can you imagine an apple tree crying out, "Oh, Lord, please bring forth apples from my life?" An apple tree doesn't have to pray to bear apples. It *has* to bring forth the life that is in it; this is the act for which it was created and it should not have to strain to produce. Fruit should come naturally. When we are in the will of God, *knowing* the will of God for our lives, we will bring forth fruit, the kind of fruit God wants each of us to bear.

By knowing the will of God, we *increase in the knowledge* of God and we are *strengthened* with all might according to His glorious power. That is strength!

Christians often complain of their weakness, rather than glory in their available strength. "It takes all the power I have just to stay right with God," they say. "Please pray for me. I need more joy and victory in my life." Sure I could pray, but ten minutes later they would feel down again. If they would seek to know God's will for their lives and stay in that will, they would be *strengthened* with all power, according to His glorious might, for the attaining of all *steadfastness* and *patience, joyously.*

When you *know* you are in the will of God, you can stand almost any hardship. The trouble arises when we are not sure a particular thing is God's will for us. Then there is confusion inside, and patience goes out the door. The Greek word for patience is *hupomone,* and freely translated it means "to remain standing after everyone else has collapsed." We have all known people who have gone through great trials and hardships, yet have exhibited great joy, vitality, and victory through it all. They can do it, because somehow they have come to know that it was God's will for them and they thank Him for it, joyfully.

Giving Thanks

When you *know* the will of God, you can give thanks to the Father in all circumstances. The Bible tells us to give thanks in *everything* (Eph. 5:20), that means while you are *going through* hardship -- not just after it is over. I have learned to practice that, giving thanks at times when the circumstances were anything but good. I say, "Father, I thank You for this. I thank You for Your will, I thank You for *all* things, in Christ Jesus, because You do not permit accidents to come into my life."

I do not believe in accidents; I cannot believe in luck, and I know the devil cannot pull a fast one while God is not looking. If God has a hand in everything that happens to me, I am going to thank Him for it, even if it does not make much sense to me at the moment. I have learned that God knows more about it than I do.

Paul speaks of "giving thanks to the Father, who has qualified us [the original meaning is *capable*] to share in the inheritance of the saints in light. For He delivered us from the domain of darkness, and transferred us to the kingdom of His beloved Son" (Col. 1:12-13). Paul is not saying *maybe!* He just says God has already made us capable, in Jesus Christ, to be partakers of our inheritance. This is not a promise about life after death. *It is valid now, in this present life.*

Perfect and Complete

How much of God's will are we capable of knowing and doing? Surely we frail and fallible human beings can only hope to begin to live up to just a small part of God's perfect plan for our lives.

But look at what Paul writes in Colossians 4:12, "Epaphras, who is one of your number, a bondslave of Jesus Christ, sends you his greetings, always laboring earnestly for you in his prayers, that you may stand *perfect* and *fully assured* (complete) in all the will of God." Paul prayed that we should know and do all of God's will for our life.

Each of us should earnestly ask, "Father, what do You want for my life and my family? What do You want for my finances, my capabilities, and my talents? All that I have and all that I am? I want to know and completely do Your will for me."

It is possible for us to know and do all the will of God for our lives. But how do we go about it? What is the next step?

The formula is found in Romans 12:1-2. "I urge you therefore, brethren, by the mercies of God, to present your bodies a living and holy sacrifice, acceptable to God, which is your spiritual service of worship. And do not be conformed to this world, but be transformed by the renewing of your mind, that you may prove what the will of God is, that which is good and acceptable and perfect."

Paul says that we should be *transformed* by the renewing of our mind. The word "transformed" is the same word used to describe what happened to Jesus on the Mount of Transfiguration. The disciples saw Jesus with Moses and Elijah. As He was transfigured, His whole countenance was changed by the glory of God. That is what Paul wants for us, that our minds be "transfigured" by the glory of God. We need to learn to *think differently* from how we ever thought before. The *ability* to *know* the will of God requires a change - the renewing of our minds.

J.B. Phillips translates the passage this way: "With eyes wide open to the mercies of God, I beg you, my brothers, as an act of intelligent worship, to give him your bodies, as a living sacrifice, consecrated to him and acceptable by him. Don't let the world around you squeeze you into its own mold, but *let God remold* your minds from within, so that you may prove in practice that the plan of God for you is good, meets all his demands and moves toward the goal of true maturity."

When God remolds our minds, we will think differently. We will see things in a different light. We will not interpret things the way we used to. There will be a difference in our understanding.

Imagine a little boy looking through a knothole in the fence at a parade going by on the street. He can see just a little bit of the parade at a time. If he sees a clown, he is full of joy. If he sees a lion, he is afraid. If there is a space between the band and the acrobats, he may even think the parade is over. And if someone stands in front of the knothole, he sees nothing. It is a very frustrating experience since he evaluates the parade only on the basis of what he sees (or cannot see) at that moment.

Then there is a voice calling his name. His older brother has climbed up on top of the roof and says, "Come on up. You can see much better from here!"

The little boy scampers up on the rooftop and from there he can see the whole length of the street below. He can see the beginning of the parade, the middle of it, and the end. It is wonderful. He is seeing things in a new perspective and it is not at all the way it looked through the knothole in the fence.

When we look at life through a knothole, we can see only what is right before our eyes, viewing and evaluating circumstances on the basis of the here and now. I see only that my wife is sick, my bankbook is empty, and my car needs a new alternator. This is the short look at life. God can see that too, but ever so much more. When we get away from the knothole and take the place where we rightfully belong, we will see things from a new perspective too. This is looking at circumstances as God sees them-- taking the long look.

Keep Looking Down

In Ephesians 2:6 Paul described where we belong: "And raised us up with Him, and seated us with Him in the heavenly places, in Christ Jesus."

A sign on a man's desk said, "Keep looking down." We see plenty of signs saying, "Keep looking up," but never one like that. When asked what the sign meant, the man said, "I used to be on earth, looking up. Now I am seated with Christ in heavenly places and I'm looking down! The view from up here is quite different."

I find myself praying, "Father, help me to see people and things as You see them."

God's Ways

God's viewpoint is not like ours. In Isaiah 55:8-9 we read, "'For My thoughts are not your thoughts, neither are your ways My ways', declares the Lord. 'For as the heavens are higher than the earth, so are My ways higher than your ways, and My thoughts than your thoughts.'"

A few years ago a woman I know in Wisconsin gave her heart to Christ and accepted Him as her Savior. That night she read in her Bible, "Believe in the Lord Jesus, and you shall be saved, you and your household" (Acts 16:31). She dropped to her knees and claimed the latter part of this verse as a promise that the Lord would save her husband. She was sure she knew just how it would happen. Her husband would come along with her to church. He would go forward and accept the Lord.

But her husband happened to hear her while she prayed. He became furious. "Shut up, woman! Do not put any of that religious stuff on me!"

So she came back to church the next night and complained, "I do not understand it. Ever since I started praying for my husband he has gotten worse."

God's ways are *not* like your ways. The man who is angry is closer to God than the man who is indifferent. Revelation 3:15-16 reads, "I would that you were cold or hot. So because you are lukewarm . . . I will spit you out of My mouth." Because she had claimed her promise, her husband was already closer than he was before, he just didn't realize it.

When you begin to pray for someone to accept Christ, you have to realize that God will do it *His* way. Whether he finds Christ in church, in his own living room, or while he is out fishing is none of your business!

Unless we experience the transformation of our thinking, we can never understand the full will of God. As humans we are always trying to read our will into it. Often we try to tell God how to work.

God will not permit Himself to be put into a box where we can anticipate His every move. He is sovereign and does what He wants and in the manner He desires. He is the King of the universe and not subject to our earthly or logical formulas. He refuses to permit us to anticipate Him or to "help Him" figure out how to do things.

Freedom to Receive

In Romans 12:2 Paul gives us the practical outline for mind renewal. First, he says *"do not."* Do not let the world squeeze you into its mold. Do not be conformed to this age. That means we must refuse to permit our thinking to follow the pattern of this world.

We are living in the days of mass media and it is hard to be the only family on the block without Nintendo or a jacuzzi. One definition of "yuppies" was *Yes Under Peer Pressure I Eat Sushi!* New fads are sweeping our nation every week. Long hair, short hair, pop and heavy metal music, new and improved everything. What is happening? It is my personal opinion that this is how the world is being brainwashed in preparation for national manipulation and Madison Avenue psychosis. Refuse to let your mind be captivated, conformed, or squeezed into the mold of this world!

Now a positive step: Let your mind be renewed; let God remold your mind from within. *Invite* the changing of your mind. *Embrace* the transforming work of the Holy Spirit. *Say* to God, "Here's my mind, Lord, my old habitual thoughts; take them and give me a new mind. Let that mind which was in Christ be in me."

That is a scriptural prayer. In Philippians 2:5 Paul says, "Have this attitude in yourselves which was also in Christ Jesus."

As we pray earnestly, God begins to remold our minds. He enables us to think the thoughts of Christ. We begin to see things as God sees them.

In Romans 12:1, Paul tells us how to do it. By deliberately giving ourselves, our bodies, a living sacrifice to God, we open the door for God's transforming power to sweep through our entire being.

We know that the Holy Spirit is a gentleman. He never forces His entry into our lives. He must be invited. The transforming of our beings into the perfect image of God *does not happen automatically.* Some Christians appear to think that once they have invited Jesus Christ at the time of salvation, He takes care of all the rest. But the *initiative* remains ours. Otherwise, it would not have been necessary for Paul to urge the Roman Christians to give themselves, their bodies, as an act of *intelligent* worship (that is, as a deliberate, well-thought-out act of commitment, not an emotional, frenzied self-sacrifice), a *living* sacrifice. Strangely we seem more eager to die for Jesus Christ than to live for Him. Be a living sacrifice, He says, daily dying to your selfish motives and desires. God wants a practical, deliberate, daily surrender of our lives, our bodies, so that He may use us. We must pray, "Here I am, Lord, all of me. Remake me, use me this day, Lord."

When God begins to remold our minds from within, we may find ourselves at odds with the world in a new way. Jesus said, "You are those who justify yourselves in the sight of men, but God knows your hearts; for that which is highly esteemed among men is *detestable* in the sight of God" (Luke 16:15). This means that sometimes you are going to stand quite alone against an issue that everybody else may think of highly.

There is a new principle here: *What man acclaims as the answer is often the very opposite of what God wants to do.* Man says, "What we need is a brand new, three-million-dollar sanctuary with padded pews. *Then* the people will come to church!"

Is that God's solution?

There were two or three million Jews who all wanted to go back to Egypt when they came to the edge of the Red Sea. But Moses said, "Oh no you don't because God says we are going *this* way!" Had they called a church business meeting and taken a vote, the count would have been two million to one. The Israelites were looking through a "knothole," while Moses was up on top of the house. With an expanded vision and a transformed mind, Moses could see the entire parade route across the Red Sea, beyond the wilderness, and into the Promised Land. The democratic process is not always the best way, especially when folks do not have the "mind of Christ" and are looking through knotholes when they should be seeking a higher view.

When you allow God to renew your mind, the change that takes place brings you into a new and glorious liberty where you will be able to walk with Jesus and find yourself able to make decisions in the light of God's eternal purpose. You begin to know what it is to stand firm and not be influenced by every new doctrine, idea, or fad (cf. Eph. 4:14). You are free to receive guidance from God.

CHAPTER
5
OUTSIDE GOD'S WILL

How do we know whether we are in the will of God or out of it?

We have taken our first steps toward learning to recognize the guiding hand of God in our personal lives. We have seen and confessed our own rebellion and made a deliberate commitment of our lives to God in Christ. We have taken Paul's advice in Romans 12:1-2 and given our physical bodies as a living sacrifice to God. We recognize that one of the results of that move is a gradual change in our very thinking process as God begins to remold our minds from within. So now, with our new perspective, we stop to take another look at ourselves and our surroundings.

Symptoms are Important

In order to find out *where* we are in the will of God, it is sometimes helpful to ask ourselves *how* we are. Deuteronomy 28:65-67 gives us a list of symptoms. *Symptoms* is a good word because we all know what it means in medical terms. When we have a persistent pain, we call it a symptom. It tells us that something is wrong. We recognize the symptom as a signal for us to do something about it. Maybe we have an injured leg, an infected appendix, or an abscessed tooth.

A symptom calls for a diagnosis and then for action. Some people live with symptoms and do nothing about them. They get so used to an aching tooth or a sore back that they think it is normal to feel that way. This is called *accommodation.*

There are many Christians who live with the symptoms of being out of God's will and think that is normal. The writer of Deuteronomy says, "You shall find *no ease* and there shall be *no rest* for the sole of your foot; but the Lord will give you there *a trembling heart, failing of eyes* [from disappointment of hope], *fainting of mind* and *languishing of spirit.* Your life shall *hang in doubt* before you; day and night you shall be *worried,* and have *no assurance* of your life. In the morning you shall say, Would it were evening! and at evening you shall say, Would it were morning! because of the *anxiety* and *dread* of your [mind and] heart, and the sights which you shall *see* with your [own] eyes" (Deut. 28:65-67 Amplified).

Look at the symptoms within you and around you. Uneasiness! Have you taken a good look at our teenagers lately? They can't do anything without noise - television, walkman's, and CD's blaring while they do their homework. When you try to turn off the noisemakers they say, "Please, Dad, I can't concentrate when it is quiet!"

Restlessness! A fainting or sorrowing of mind! Depression! Do you feel it? What do you do about it? Do you take anti-depressant pills, tranquilizers or pray for God to take away your worries?

Uncertainty. Fearfulness. Anxiety. Every time you hear the fire engine or the police siren, do you have a queasy feeling in your stomach, fear it is your house, your kids? What if a burglar comes tonight? What if a famine strikes? What if we have an all-out war or a bad flu epidemic? I hear Christians talk of worry and I cringe. They are exhibiting symptoms of being out of the center of God's will.

Spiritual Bondage

A retired medical missionary lived by herself in a little cottage right in the middle of a ghetto in a Florida town. There had been some lootings, burnings, and demonstrations around her. Every time it happened, her friends asked, "Aren't you afraid of being alone at night? Maybe you ought to get a big watchdog!"

The lady always smiled and shook her head saying, "There is no safer place in the whole world than in the center of God's will. He placed me here and He is my mighty fortress."

All around us we see men's hearts failing them for fear, lack of assurance, and discontent. What are the final symptoms? The Bible tells us, "And the Lord shall bring you into Egypt again with ships, by the way about which I said to you, You shall never see it again; and there you shall be sold to your enemies for bondmen and bondwomen, and no man shall buy you" (Deut. 28:68 Amplified). In other words, if we allow these symptoms to persist, they will lead us into *final spiritual bondage.*

Calamities and Adversities

Where do the symptoms come from? Most of us blame them on circumstances. We say, "I lie awake worrying at night because I lost my job. If I could only get another job, I wouldn't worry." Now seen from a human point of view, that is a perfectly reasonable explanation for our *anxiety* and sleeplessness; so we get a few sleeping pills to carry us over the rough spot. If we are a Christian, we might call the prayer-chain in our church and have them pray for a new job. We might even talk to the minister and have him pray for our "nerves." However, verse 65 in the chapter we just read says, "The *Lord* will give you there a trembling heart. . . ."

From our new perspective, we should take another look at our unemployment. "Did *You* allow that to happen, Lord? Did You want me to discover my own anxiety and look for a deeper cause - knowing this was far more important than keeping my job?"

Since God began to bring about a change in my way of thinking, I do not look at the difficulties in my life the way I used to. I am beginning to realize they are there to expose symptoms: pride, rebellion, fear, insecurity, and lack of assurance. We need these things to crowd us into God. I wish we were all so obedient that such hardships would not be necessary, but we are not. And so, I have started to thank God when He allows difficulty to come into my life.

If God did not have use for the devil, He would have bound him and cast him into the pit thousands of years ago. Why, then does God permit him to exist? Simply because Satan is the one who creates the needs that drive us to Jesus. When things are fine or in a rut, who needs Jesus? But when suddenly the children are sick, and the transmission fails on our car, we are back on our knees, praying.

"Needs"

We make a mistake when we call our symptoms "needs" and simply pray that God remove them. Like the pain from a ruptured appendix or the dizziness from a brain tumor, symptoms are there for a reason. God intends for us to let Him expose the deeper cause and bring healing. Relief from pain could be the most tragic thing that ever happened, unless the cause was removed. *"It will go away"* can be four dangerous words.

Most of us are escape artists. We will use any excuse to keep from facing up to our own failings. Modern psychology has provided us several new escape mechanisms. Many of us have been influenced by some aspect of the Freudian theories about our psychological problems.

Ego Problems

Freud described our ego (self) as being trapped somewhere between the id (our natural appetites and desires) and the superego (our conscience). Freud said the id is an expression of what we "want" to do and these wants are regulated by the superego which reminds us what we have been taught that we ought or ought not to do. Problems arise when the conflicts between our wants and cannots become too strong. In psychological circles these conflicts are known as "frustrations." In Freudian thinking, the solution lies in removing the restrictions so that the ego (self) will not become warped by guilt complexes. This is called "adjusting."

In the Navy, I had a shipmate who was about to crack up. As the ship's medic, I took him to the base psychiatrist in Japan. He spent about forty-five minutes in the doctor's office. When he came out he said, "Bob, do you know what the doctor told me to do? He said I should go ashore, get the best prostitute in Japan, get cock-eyed drunk, and I'd be all right in the morning."

My friend took the doctor's advice. Did his guilt feelings increase or decrease?

Two months later he had a total breakdown on board ship. With a loaded gun he retreated to a forward hold and had to be removed by force and committed to a mental institution. He did not need to adjust his superego disciplines to the animal drives of his id. Rather, he needed his id transformed by the power of God. Sad to say, this is the one thing the psychiatrist deemed impossible. As a Freudian theorist, he read the "symptom" as the cause and prescribed "adjustment" as the cure. What my shipmate really needed was a good old-fashioned dose of repentance.

Reality Therapy

Magazines and books on child-rearing and education often teach that young people must be allowed freedom to express themselves or their personalities will be warped. Today we are reaping the consequences of such teachings in an increased lawlessness, lack of respect for property, authority, and individuals. The so-called new morality teaches we are not responsible for what we do - if we have the desire to do it. It must be legal or God would not have given us the desire in the first place, the new school teaches.

Our mental hospitals and psychiatric clinics are full of miserable people who have been told that their problems arise from excessive guilt feelings imposed on them by the narrow, puritanical teachings they received at home or in Sunday school. While this is a real possibility, ordinarily and in the majority of cases, it is the very opposite of what the *cause* should be determined to be. Millions of Americans consume tons of tranquilizers and drink gallons of alcohol to ease their symptoms while they plunge headlong into more excessive self-expression to find release from their guilt complexes.

Fortunately, the last few years have seen the beginning of a reversal in thought among leading psychiatrists. A theory called *Reality Therapy* continues to gain recognition. Christians will say that the "new theory" is as old as the Bible. It teaches that we are *responsible* for what we do and that feelings of guilt are not only normal but healthy. In fact, it is abnormal not to feel guilty when we oppose and rebel against God. And the built-in pressures of guilt feelings are designed to drive us back to the source so that we can make the wrong right.

As Christians we recognize, of course, that God's grace is the answer to our guilt and that confession will bring release and restoration. Unconfessed sin is like a festering sore. A Band-Aid or a tranquilizer will not bring healing, only a temporary hiding or escape from the symptom.

In Reality Therapy, psychiatrists recognize that wrong actions give rise to guilt feelings. For example, if I am supposed to be at work at eight o'clock and I sleep until five minutes of eight, I get to the office at 8:15 and have bad feelings inside. I don't want to see the boss. He says, "Bob, how come you were late this morning?" I say, "Well, uh, er, there was a traffic jam." The bad feelings inside me increase. First I did something wrong, then I lied to cover it up. Before I know it, I am getting in deeper and deeper. I get a headache. I'm grumpy all day and that night I cannot go to sleep without a sleeping pill.

Now the quickest way to get rid of all this before it builds up and becomes worse is to swallow my pride and rectify the situation by telling my boss the truth. Granted, this may cause a new set of problems, but at least I can go to work combating them because they are founded on truth. Problems built on a lie can never be solved until the lie is acknowledged and corrected.

The Bible story about the prodigal son is a classic example of the repentance experience. The son wasted his inheritance and when the symptoms became bad enough, he returned to his father, confessed, asked forgiveness, and was restored.

David's Instructions

In Psalm 32 David said, "How blessed is he whose transgression is forgiven, whose sin is covered! I acknowledged my sin to Thee, and my iniquity I did not hide; I said, 'I will confess my transgressions to the Lord, and Thou didst forgive the guilt of my sin'" (Ps. 32:1,5). What was David's sin? He had committed adultery, murder, and lied about it. When the pressures became too great he confessed, acknowledged his sin to God, and received forgiveness and release. That is Reality Therapy that ran its full course.

Escape into Freud

Why do Americans consume more medicine than any other nation? We are trying to escape facing ourselves.

The first escape artist was Adam. God came after Adam and said, "What have you done?" Adam said, "It was that woman you gave me; she is to blame." Then God asked Eve and she became the second escape artist. She blamed the serpent. This escape process is almost always at the root of our emotional distress!

When things do not go right in our lives, we blame everybody else. Maybe the Bible is wrong. Maybe the pastor who prayed for me didn't have enough faith. Maybe God is not listening. Maybe it is a spiritual attack. Maybe it is because my mother forced me to eat lima beans when I was a child. We blame everybody but ourselves. Because we are Freudian oriented, we fall in love with the church youth worker. She is married and the mother of two children, but we still say, "I can't help it; every time I see her in church I get funny feelings. I just can't help it."

You better help it! The Bible says *we* are responsible and Jesus does not mince His words about adultery, "But I say to you, that everyone who *looks* on a woman to lust for her has committed adultery with her already in his heart" (Matt. 5:28). Those words would not be in the Book if God had made us incapable of disciplining our feelings.

Freudian psychology would lead us to believe that an alcoholic is sick. However, the Bible says drunkenness is sin! It is a chemical escape from reality. In Alcoholics Anonymous they have a twelve-step program to sobriety. The first step is to confess you are an alcoholic. The second step is to turn to God. That is Reality Therapy. In Christian terms, we call it repentance and faith.

Homosexual Deliverance

"Homosexuality is a condition that cannot be helped," says our modern generation, clamoring for the "rights" of the homosexuals. But the Bible calls it sin and says we are to refuse it and be delivered from it.

Once there was a young man leading the song-service in a large church in New York City. Suddenly he stopped and said, "People, tonight is a very crucial night for me." Everyone was quiet watching him. He went on, "If the Lord Jesus does not help me tonight, I do not know where I will ever get help. I'm homosexual."

For years he had excused himself saying, "My mother overshadowed me. My father deserted us. It is *their* fault I am this way." But that night he faced it "right on." He confessed. He repented. He did not want to go on living that way, and he was helped. Someone there in the church prayed for him, and God delivered him. He still had to walk out the implications of a life holy before the Lord. Not all problems are solved easily, but the *principle* and the route to release is the same for everyone.

Old-Fashioned Restitution

When we face ourselves and bring our problems to God, we get release. But most of us have developed a habit pattern of getting *around* our guilt feelings. We pray or ask others to pray for us to relieve the symptoms, but nothing happens. Symptoms do not need to be relieved; *sources* need to be healed. And prayer is not to be used as an escape from the necessity for repentance from sin.

It is an interesting fact that the people who *do not* get healed at healing services are most often Christians. God is dealing with them and they are seeking to escape. God wants them to repent, and they want the symptoms to ease. No wonder many Christians are confused, uneasy, and discontented. They have developed elaborate, impenetrable habit patterns of escape.

We are promised joy and peace in Jesus. If we do not have joy and peace, we had better take another look at the reason. The Apostle Paul says the kingdom of God is righteousness - then peace and joy (Rom. 14:17).

You can cheat on your income tax and carry resentment against your mother-in-law, and still be a Christian. But you can't cheat on your taxes, resent your mother-in-law and still have peace and happiness as a fruit of the Holy Spirit.

Once, while praying and telling God how much I loved Him and wanted to serve Him, I experienced the principles of guidance we are now learning. I had been discharged from the Navy and had been a Christian only a short time. The thought in my mind was unmistakably the voice of God saying, "Do you remember all that medicine you stole from the Navy?" It was like the voice of a stern and concerned Father. Since I had accumulated a small "hospital" at home, I began to squirm.

"Yes, Lord."

"I want you to take it all back!"

"But, Lord," I argued, "if I take it back, they'll send me to the penitentiary and I'll never get out."

"Pack it up and take it back!" was the immediate response.

I packed up two shopping bags full of medicine, medical instruments, bandages, and drugs and went to the Navy base. Walking up to the Officer of the Day, I said, "Sir, I have business with the Medical Officer."

The officer didn't even look in my shopping bags. He said, "Sign right here." I got through the gates and sank down on the curb, my stomach in a flutter.

"Thank You, Lord," I said, "for getting me through that gate."

I walked down the hall, toward the Medical Officer's station, and a fellow called my name through an open door.

"Bob, where are you going?" It was a civilian friend I had known previously. I told him I had two shopping bags full of stolen articles and I was bringing them back.

"What's the matter with you?" he said amazed. "Everyone steals stuff like this from the Navy." I stayed and talked to him for two and a half hours about Jesus Christ and what He had done in my life. Finally, the fellow said, "I am in charge of all medical supplies. I will put all these things back on the shelves for you. You go home. Guys like you are dangerous to have around."

We put all the medicine back in proper order, and I walked out of that base floating on air. I thought if God can invade a Navy base like that, He can do anything. If I had refused to take the medicine back, I would have started a dangerous pattern of escape that would have led to negative spiritual symptoms and uselessness in God's kingdom.

Ask God to help you face yourself, uncover old habit patterns, and reveal your escape mechanisms and idiosyncrasies. We all have them. You will find God intruding into your daily life in a way that will keep you constantly on your toes.

One day I parked my car illegally, thinking I could get away with it, but when I came back after a few minutes, there was a ticket tucked under my winshield wiper. I said, "Lord, why didn't You protect me? I'm a minister and I work for You, Lord."

"Does that give you a license to break the law?" the Lord responded.

The next day, while driving home, a traffic light turned yellow. I sped up and flashed under it. Then I looked in the rear view mirror. You guessed it. A patrol car was right behind me - his lights blinking.

"God, what's the matter with You?" I murmured as I pulled to the curb. "I don't have the money to pay fines. I'm Your servant and would much rather give the money to missions than to the courts."

"Who do you think brought that patrol car behind you?" the Lord asked. "Don't you understand what I am trying to teach you?"

"Yes, Lord, I understand. Thank You for the ticket."

God will not permit escape mechanisms anymore. He wants to bring us to full release.

There are Christians who have escaped all their lives. They have never faced themselves, their marriage, or the Word of God. When the symptoms begin to pressure you in any area of your life, you need to know how to respond. God is presenting you an opportunity to face yourself. For unless you are willing to be honest with yourself and with God, it is most difficult to move on in God's purpose for your life.

CHAPTER
6
CONDITIONAL GUIDANCE

Unconditional Guidance

There is a fundamental difference between unconditional guidance and conditional guidance. The first is present in the lives of all believers. God acts in sovereignty regardless of *our* present attitude.

Cyrus

A prime example of unconditional guidance is found in Isaiah 45. God says to Cyrus, "I will go before you and make the rough places smooth; I will shatter the doors of bronze, and cut through their iron bars. For the sake of Jacob My servant, and Israel My chosen one, I have also called you by your name; I have given you a title of honor *though you have not known Me.* I am the Lord, and there is no other; besides Me there is no God. I will gird you, *though you have not known me*"(Isa. 45:2,4-5).

Cyrus was king of Persia. In the book of Ezra, we read that in the first year of his reign, God stirred up Cyrus's spirit so that he made a proclamation throughout all his domain saying that the Lord God of heaven had given him all the nations of the earth and charged him to build Him a house at Jerusalem. Cyrus then allowed all who were called "God's people" to go back to Jerusalem to rebuild the Temple. He told others to help with gifts of silver, gold, and freewill offerings for the house of God.

God was with Cyrus. He called him His shepherd who would perform all His pleasure. This was even *before* Cyrus knew God. Yet God's sovereign hand had begun to arrange the circumstances and lay all the nations at Cyrus's feet. Why did God do all this? Isaiah 45:4 says it was, "For the sake of Jacob My servant, and Israel My chosen one." And Ezra adds additional perspective saying, "in order to fulfill the word of the Lord by the mouth of Jeremiah" (Ezra 1:1).

God was using Cyrus to bring about the promise He had given His elect, Israel, through Jeremiah. Israel had been a rebellious, disobedient people, resisting God's guidance and seeking after other gods. As a result, they were carried away captive to Babylon by Nebuchadnezzar. But through Jeremiah, God had spoken and said that after seventy years He would turn again their captivity, bring them back to Jerusalem, and rebuild the Temple. Had the Israelites obeyed God in the first place and turned from their wicked and rebellious ways when they were first warned through the words of the prophet, they would have escaped captivity. God was acting out His sovereign plan for the Israelites regardless of their attitude. This is *unconditional* guidance.

God's unconditional guidance is in operation in our lives because God honors His Word, and because we are His people. It is not that we are deserving, but because Christ redeemed us on the Cross at Calvary.

It is significant that God had to use Cyrus, a foreign king, to guide His people back to Jerusalem. The Israelites,

God's own people, didn't know the joy of walking in fellowship with God.

How often, after having stumbled through a series of circumstances, grumbling all the way, completely oblivious to God's hand do we find ourselves in the place where God wants us? If we had listened to God in the first place, we would have gone joyfully, avoiding the detours and painful delays.

Conditional Guidance

Apart from God's unconditional guidance, there is also guidance that comes only when we comply with certain conditions. This is *conditional guidance* and is described in Isaiah 58:10-11: "And if you give yourself to the hungry, and satisfy the desire of the afflicted, then your light will rise in darkness, and your gloom will become like midday. And the Lord *will continually guide you,* and satisfy your desire in scorched places, and give strength to your bones; and you will be like a watered garden, and like a spring of water whose waters do not fail."

Selfishness

What would keep God from making good His promise of guiding us continually? God says there are certain conditions man must meet before he can receive *specific* guidance. Actions such as giving ourselves to the hungry and satisfying the desires of the afflicted are some of these conditions.

Selfishness is a hindrance to divine guidance. Selfishness produces a hardness in us which the Lord is constantly warning us about. For example, suppose the Holy Spirit urges us to give ten dollars to our unemployed friend.

"Not me, Lord. The kids need new shoes and I might be laid off next." The point is not the ten dollars. God could provide our friend with ten dollars from some other source. But a dangerous hardness develops in our spirit when we resist the leading of God; therefore *compassion* becomes essential in our lives.

Stubbornness

Stubbornness is another hindrance to guidance.

Psalm 32:8-9 reads, "I will instruct you and teach you in the way which you should go; I will counsel you with My eye upon you. Do not be as the horse or as the mule which have no understanding, whose trappings include bit and bridle to hold them in check, otherwise they will not come near to you." There are many Christians who *know* what God wants of them but they simply refuse to obey. A willingness to obey is a primary condition for guidance. John 7:17 says, "If any man is willing to do His will, he shall know of the teaching, whether it is of God, or whether I speak from Myself." Jesus reassures us that if we are willing to do God's will, we will not be led astray. I have heard people use the excuse, "I don't know if it is God's will or not." If you really are willing to do God's will, you *can* know! Chances are there is a stubborn streak hidden somewhere which prevents you from doing what you ought to do. Stubbornness can prevent us from even seeking the will of God. Are you a "rugged individualist"? Stubborn individuals say, "I like my plans the way they are, I don't want God to interfere." There is a place for individuality, but in our relationship to God, we must be yielded.

Disobedience

Disobedience, that is, knowing unmistakably what God wants you to do, but refusing to do it also hinders guidance. This is dangerous business, and the Bible is full of examples of what happened to men and women who deliberately hardened their hearts and set themselves to go against God's orders. The list is long and includes both the "enemies" of God as well as God's own people. You could begin with the first family on earth and see that original sin came into the world through a deliberate act of disobedience. Moses disobeyed when he smote the rock for water in the desert of Zin. The Israelites disobeyed the command to go in and possess the land. Samson disobeyed and lost not only his strength, but his life. Saul disobeyed by consulting a witch, and the anointing of God was replaced with a curse. David deliberately committed adultery, then murder, and lost his joy as well as the presence of the Holy Spirit. The list goes on and on, and the result of deliberate disobedience is always the same - the loss of God's conditional guidance plus other penalties that suit the case. When God says, "Don't," we had better not. When He says, "Do," we had better. We have no one to blame but ourselves.

Insincerity

Insincerity stands between us and God's guidance.

There are people who pray loudly, "O God, I want to do Your will. Just tell me Lord, and I will do it." But internally they have their own agenda and a personal preset course with no intention of taking God's advice.

Jeremiah 42 records the incident of the remnant of Judah coming to Jeremiah and begging him to seek the Lord for guidance. "Whatever God tells us to do, we will do," they said. Ten days later the word of God came to Jeremiah, and he prophesied saying, "Do not go into Egypt. Therefore you should now clearly understand that you will die by the sword, by famine, and by pestilence. . ." (Jer. 42:19,22).

Did the leaders of Judah rejoice in the Lord for His guidance? No, they turned against Jeremiah and said, "You're a liar. That is not what God said. We will go to Egypt regardless of what you say!" They never intended to change their mind. They were determined to go to Egypt and sent Jeremiah to seek God's Word. They wanted His approval to do what they had already decided to do.

How many times have we done just that! We have decided what we want to do, and we want to bolster our decision by getting the approval of other Christians or the pastor. We search the Bible for verses that will support our decision. We pray, "O Lord, show us the way," and then we seek the wise counsel of others. If we run up against disapproval we say, "They are just not spiritual enough to understand God's will in this." *We take only the opinion and advice that agrees with our pre-set decision.* That is insincerity. We did not mean it when we asked our Christian friends. We did not mean it when we prayed. Our insincerity and deceitfulness stand like a wall between us and guidance from God.

Impatience

Impatience is another stumbling block.

Habakkuk 2:3 deals with this, "For the vision is yet for the appointed time; it hastens toward the goal, and it will not fail. Though it tarries, wait for it; for it will certainly come, it will not delay."

A classic example of impatience, interfering with God's guidance, is found in I Samuel 13. Saul had been told to wait seven days before going into battle. At the end of this time Samuel was to appear and offer up a sacrifice to God. Seven days passed and Samuel had not arrived. Saul was impatient. He saw the enemy all around. His own troops were getting worried, and he decided to take matters into his own hands and proceed with the sacrifice. No sooner had he done it, than Samuel appeared on the scene.

"You have acted foolishly," Samuel said to Saul, "you have not kept the commandment of the Lord your God. But now your kingdom shall not endure. The Lord has sought out for Himself a man after His own heart, and the Lord has appointed him as ruler over His people . . ." (I Sam. 13:13,14). Saul lost a kingdom because he did not wait as he had been instructed.

Again and again in the Bible we are told that waiting on God is a necessity, a virtue, a source of strength. Yet impatience is probably the failure which occurs most often. We pray about a new job, the salvation of someone we love, the solution to a problem, and God gives us a wonderful assurance and peace. We know our prayers are being answered. We have perfect peace - for an hour - but then we start nagging, "Lord, You promised. Why aren't You doing it?" Our response is to busy ourselves arranging circumstances and manipulating people. "If You don't do something about it, we will just go ahead and have a revival in our church anyway."

God operates on split-second timing and He is never late. When the conditions are right and God's appointed time is here, God moves. By running ahead of Him, we can seriously harm ourselves and others.

Once I prayed for a different car. I needed a more dependable one and felt the confidence to ask the Lord for it. Day after day went by and I got impatient. Finally I decided I had waited long enough and marched into a used-car agency downtown.

"I would like to look at a car," I said.

"Certainly," the salesman said with a grin. "We'll fix you right up!"

He sure did. I had no peace when I looked at that car, but by then I was impatient, stubborn, and hard of hearing.

"I'll take it," I said and drove out. The car gave me nothing but trouble, and I was still making payments long after the car was hauled to the junkyard.

Self-Sufficiency

Perhaps the most dangerous hindrance to guidance is *self-sufficiency*, and by nature we say, "Show me and I will believe." God says, "Believe and you will see!"

Proverbs 3:5-7 gives us this piece of advice, "Trust in the Lord with all your heart, and do not lean on your own understanding. In all your ways acknowledge Him, and He will make your paths straight. Do not be wise in your own eyes; fear the Lord and turn away from evil."

One of God's greatest hindrances in His servants is self-sufficiency. Much of God's dealing with us is to destroy this. It manifests itself in this way: "You show me the first time, Lord, and I will take it from there."

The life of dependence is humbling, and to deal with self-sufficiency, God keeps us in a *slight state of crisis* most of the time. An associate of mine who knows the life of dependency upon God needed twelve hundred dollars. After much prayer, the money was remarkably supplied. He gave a heavy sigh of relief to which God responded, "Is this a sigh of relief because the money has been supplied - or because you no longer have to trust Me?" It was a rebuke well needed.

Pride

Pride is a real but subtle hindrance to guidance.

For years God dealt with me about becoming a Christian behind the steering wheel. I had always considered myself an expert driver and felt I did not need any guidance from God on that score. Then one day I read a report by a trooper in the Canadian Royal Mounted Police that said most accidents were caused not by faulty brakes, speed, or even alcohol; but because most drivers subtly felt they were much better drivers than they were in reality. The trooper was saying that false pride led drivers to take chances and do unwise and unsafe things because of their blinding conceit which led them to say, "When I am at the wheel everything is okay." Little by little God reduced my pride and self-sufficiency and taught me to trust Him and His evaluation of every road situation.

Many people who have degrees in business, psychology, engineering, or medicine trust God in the "religious" areas of their life, that is, in going to church on Sunday, making moral decisions about lying or cheating, or even tithing their money. But when it comes to their own specialty - business, psychology, engineering, or medicine - "pride" causes them to reject God's guidance.

God never expects us to be robots. His guidance most always depends upon our thinking processes. He longs for us to mature to the place that we can use our "sanctified intellect" and "understanding" to make the right decisions in following His guidance. However, God knows infinitely more than we do about *any* given subject in which we may consider ourselves experts. His desire for us is that we acknowledge Him as sovereign God and recognize our own need for Him.

Ordinarily we think that the more we learn of God's ways, the more we will be able to move with self-assurance and certainty. But in reality the more we understand, the more dependent upon God we become.

Jeremiah cried out to God: "I know, O Lord, that a man's way is not in himself; nor is it in a man who walks to direct his steps" (Jer. 10:23). Jeremiah had come to recognize his own need, and this is a primary condition for direct guidance.

A person full of pride is not willing to be taught. Only the meek can learn. Psalm 25:9 says, "He leads the humble in justice, and He teaches the humble His way."

When we depend solely on God in all areas of our life, He can meet our needs and guide us in all things. Only then can we surrender our will completely to the will of God and say with David, "I delight to do Thy will, O my God; Thy Law is within my heart" (Ps. 40:8).

The secret to the Christian life is that Christ lives within us. When Christ rules in our lives we should be able to say to Him, "My food is to do the will of Him who sent Me, and to accomplish His work" (John 4:34).

Determination

The characteristic of a *surrendered will* is a determination to set aside its own will for that of God's. Jesus prayed in Gethsemane, "Abba! Father! All things are possible for Thee; remove this cup from Me; yet not what I will, but what Thou wilt" (Mark 14:36).

A completely yielded will opens the door for increasingly direct, divine guidance in our lives.

CHAPTER
7
THREE HARBOR LIGHTS

Navigation in the Spirit

Prior to electronic navigation, a certain harbor in Italy could only be reached by sailing up a narrow channel between dangerous rocks and shoals. Over the years, many ships have been wrecked there, and navigation is extremely hazardous.

To guide the ships safely into port, three lights have been mounted on three huge poles in the harbor. When the three lights are perfectly lined up and seen as one, the ship can safely turn to begin navigation up the narrow channel. If the pilot sees two or three lights separately, he knows that he is off course and in danger! He must continue to maneuver his vessel until the lights perfectly line up before he can safely turn into the harbor.

For our safety in navigating our ship of life, God has provided three beacons to guide us. The same rules of navigation apply to us as to the harbor pilot. The three lights must be perfectly lined up as one before it is safe for us to proceed up the channel. The three harbor lights of guidance are:

1. The Word of God (objective standard)
2. The Holy Spirit (subjective witness)
3. Circumstances (divine providence)

Together they assure us that the direction and guidance we have received are from God and will lead us safely along the way that is His revealed will for us.

The Supreme Criterion

The written Word of God is the supreme criterion in all guidance. In his second epistle, Peter refers to his experience on the Mount of Transfiguration with Jesus, James, and John. Here they saw Moses and Elijah and heard the voice of God from heaven say, "This is My beloved Son with whom I am well-pleased" (II Peter 1:17).

Can you imagine what it would have been like to have been with Jesus on that mountaintop? Can you imagine what it would have been like to have seen Jesus transfigured before your very eyes and to have heard the audible voice of God with your own ears? And yet Peter says, "And so we have the prophetic word *made more sure*, to which you do well to pay attention as to a lamp shining in a dark place, until the day dawns and the morning star arises in your hearts. But know this first of all, that no prophecy of Scripture is a matter of one's own interpretation" (II Peter 1:19-20). Peter had heard the audible voice of God from heaven, yet he says that the written Word is *more sure*.

The Bible is the Word of God. Jesus Himself said, "For truly I say to you, until heaven and earth pass away, not the smallest letter or stroke shall pass away from the Law, until all is accomplished" (Matt. 5:18). He later said, "Heaven and earth will pass away, but My words will not pass away" (Luke 21:33).

The amazing thing about God's Word is that it never goes out of style. Over the last decades we have seen the remarkable changes in concepts of science as research has uncovered evidence supporting the views of the Bible. Is it interesting that as man's empirical knowledge of his nature and environment increases, the seeming gap of conflict between God's revelation in the Bible and man's knowledge of himself and of human behavior narrows rather than widens. The pseudo-scientific concept that suggests, "We can no longer accept or depend upon the truth of the Bible," simply cannot stand the close scrutiny of behavioral research.

The Bible is the *living* Word and by the mere reading of it can quicken hearts, change lives, and heal broken bodies and spirits. Jesus, who is God's Word become flesh, uses the expression, "I am the vine, you are the branches" (John 15:5). I would like to use the same illustration about the written Word of God, the Bible. The first three chapters of Genesis make up the root of the vine. To cut off the root would mean the rest of the vine would wither and die. The whole Bible stands or falls on the story of the beginning. The same is true with the story of the beginning of the life of Jesus. To say it doesn't matter whether Jesus was born of a virgin or not is like cutting the taproot of the vine but still expecting a harvest of grapes in the fall. The Bible is an organic whole.

The book of Corinthians was written in A.D. 56. That is over 1,900 years ago. What if you wanted to study electronics, automobile mechanics, medicine, or aerodynamics? Would you pick up a book written in the first century? Probably not! Most likely you would not even take seriously a textbook written fifty years ago. But the problems and solutions of the Corinthians are still applicable to us and our society today. Thus the Word of God stands as a valid criterion for human behavior today. It does indeed speak to the whole of life.

It is interesting that in the past 2000 years there has not appeared any "new" sin, i.e. one that the Scriptures has not already addressed. God has given us ". . . all things that pertain to life and godliness" (II Peter 2:3).

Misinterpreting

Can God speak to us today? Of course He can, and He does. But how can we know it is God and not demonic or perhaps our own super-heated imagination? We are able to accomplish this by measuring God's spoken Word by His written Word.

Jesus spoke directly to His disciples; yet they always seemed to misunderstand Him. He became a little exasperated with them a few times because He had to tell them things over and over again and they still did not understand what He meant. Once, when in a boat, He told the disciples, "Beware of the leaven of the Pharisees."

The disciples discussed this among themselves and then decided that Jesus was disturbed because they had forgotten to bring bread. Jesus knew what they were thinking and said that was not what He meant at all; after all, didn't they remember how He had fed the five thousand with just a couple of loaves? At last the disciples began to understand what He meant. Leaven was the dangerous doctrine of the Pharisees and Sadducees (Matt. 16:5-12).

Another time Jesus stood in front of the Temple and said, "Destroy this temple, and in three days I will raise it up" (John 2:19). Again they misinterpreted completely what He said.

Several years ago I was riding in a car with a friend when the manifest presence of the Holy Spirit seemed to fill the entire car. We had been praying, praising, and worshiping as we drove along. Suddenly the Spirit of God was so real and overwhelming that we pulled over to the side of the road and stopped. The atmosphere was supercharged with the wonderful presence of the Holy Spirit, and the voice of the Lord was distinct in my mind, "I want you to go to Peru!"

It was a dramatic and direct call. *God wants me to go to Peru immediately,* I thought. My wife and I sold all our belongings, believing that God was going to miraculously supply the needed five thousand dollars so we could fly off to Peru and minister to the Indians. We waited week after week, but still no provisions arrived. It was seven years before the Lord sent me to Peru, and even then it was not in the manner that I had expected, but as an invited teacher for an on-going ministers' training course. For five or six years we invested ourselves in Peru as the land of God's call. The outworking was certainly different than I first interpreted!

God's revelation was only partial, but I was in such a hurry that I acted as if it were complete. When I finally arrived in Peru and stood on a platform among the towering mountains of the Andes, I heard the voice of the Lord in my human spirit very distinctly again, "Now you are seeing the fulfillment of My words to you."

Standing there, I wept openly, "God, how I misinterpreted what You said to me!" God had given me the inner witness of the Holy Spirit, but I lacked the third witness, the open door of circumstances, and had almost wreaked havoc in my ministry and marriage by trying to run ahead of Him.

A Christian building contractor was talking on the telephone with another Christian friend. Suddenly the friend said, "It is the Lord's desire to bless you!" The contractor thought, *God intends to give me more money and prosper my business!* Thinking this was what "bless you" meant, he began to expand his construction business on every hand. He overextended himself financially and the bottom fell out. He was broke! He could not understand what had happened. After all, the Lord had promised to bless him.

He concluded that he had no choice but to declare bankruptcy. The Lord's voice came through loud and clear, however, "Oh, no you're not. Stay with it. You are not skipping out on a single debt. We will pay them back together."

Miraculously, one by one, God paid the bills. It took several years, but slowly the business gained profitability until he was completely out of debt. Later he told me, "I am so thankful for what God has taught me over the last few years. *He has truly blessed me.*"

Was it necessary for him to go through near bankruptcy to learn? Yes, but only because my friend did not know how to measure what he had heard with the other two criteria of God's written Word and circumstances.

Most of us completely *misunderstand* and consequently, misinterpret what God says in the first place. We often jump to the wrong conclusion instead of waiting for the other two harbor lights to line up as witnesses to give solid guidance and direction - the kind of guidance we can hold on to.

Many problems in Christianity come because we *read into* God's Word something that is not there. We get carried away by our own imaginations. Equally confusing, however, is the *removal* of portions of God's Word because it conflicts with our church tradition or dispensational teaching.

Sources of Guidance

The three harbor lights are there because guidance in real life, through real decisions, is a passage which is quite dangerous, with rocks and shoals on both sides. There are three *sources* of guidance: God, demonic, and our own spirit or imagination. As for the latter, we get all super-heated and worked up; we hear and see things, and in this state we misinterpret and often get ourselves into great difficulty.

Challenging a Leading

Someone says, "I've had a vision; I've heard a voice!" This is quite possible, but could it be false? Are we expected to follow every vision and obey every impression?

In I Corinthians 14:37 Paul says, "If anyone thinks he is a prophet or spiritual, let him recognize that the things which I write to you are the Lord's commandments." The implication is that the Holy Spirit Himself yields to and bows to the written Word. He never acts outside of or in contradiction to the Scripture which He Himself inspired. This is His own criterion so that we can recognize what is of God and what is not. Remember, when in conflict, the Holy Spirit is the One who *inspired* the Word of God in the first place.

You may have known of some people in Christian circles who have described weird visions and messages or unbiblical forms of guidance. If you attempt to speak to them, they usually bristle like porcupines.

"Are you challenging what God said to me?"

"Yes! What ever happened to the plain meaning of Scriptures?"

"I can't help what that verse says, I only *know* what God said to me!"

God never speaks in contradiction to His own written Word. He will never lead you beyond the revelation He has already given in Jesus Christ. Do not make serious decisions on the basis of one initial leading. If it is God speaking to you, the other two lights will line up in perfect agreement. It should be comforting to know that God does not require a response without waiting for those other two witnesses. There is a law in the Scriptures that "on the evidence of two or three witnesses a matter shall be confirmed" (Deut. 19:15). If a man was caught in adultery and there were two or three witnesses, he was stoned without discussion. In guidance we need the three witnesses to be sure: the Scripture in plain meaning, the inner witness of the Holy

Spirit, and outward circumstances. Either of the three taken alone can be deceptive. Wait for all three to line up. The God of the Bible never lies, but a biblical verse lifted out of context can cause serious damage.

Finger Pointing, Button Pushing & Promise Cards

There are three other forms of "effortless guidance" which, although not to be totally discounted as legitimate forms of guidance, are the kind that will turn us into spiritual pygmies. Their quick and easy approach leads us into the dangerous habit of bypassing the serious effort we need to put forth in order to find genuine guidance. I refer to them as *finger pointing, button pushing,* and *promise card boxes.*

Let me hasten to add that I know these three forms of guidance have worked under certain circumstances and on certain occasions, but I say unequivocally that a continued dependence upon them will result in deception. Whenever we make the *exceptional* form of guidance to be the normal rule, we are in difficulty.

Let us look at *finger pointing.* A young couple who felt called to the mission field and did not know where to go, opened their Bible at random, *pointed at a verse* and read, "The isles of the sea wait for thee."

They said, "That means the Lord wants us to go to one of the Pacific islands." They proceeded posthaste to put themselves on a certain Pacific island.

Six months later they were back. The wife spent some time in a mental institution and they were both broken in faith and spirit.

An equal danger lies in *button pushing*. I worked with a doctor in Toronto who had a patient who believed she had cancer - even though the laboratory procedures had proven she did not. The doctor, however, treated her and counseled her. He created the impression that he agreed with her.

After she left, I said, "You're deceiving her."

"No, she's a button-pusher," he said. "That means if I don't treat her for what *she thinks she has,* she will keep ringing doctors' doorbells until she hears what she wants to hear. Thus I give her harmless treatments while someone else would have taken advantage of her."

Sincere but careless Christians often feel guidance can be obtained by asking (button-pushing) a variety of spiritual leaders, pastors, and visiting evangelists. Often, they keep asking until someone tells them what they already wanted to hear.

The same danger lies in using a *promise box* for guidance. A box of scriptures is a good thing to have on the breakfast table and makes for uplifting and pleasant devotion, but used in guidance, it has dangerous implications. God's promises are all real, but picked out of context from a promise box they can be very misleading.

Suppose one day you are crying out to God because you have so many needs. The rent is due, and there is no money for groceries. You reach into the box for a promise. There it is, thank God, "And my God shall supply all your needs according to His riches in glory in Christ Jesus" (Phil. 4:19).

Hallelujah, you have nothing to worry about! Just wait, and the Lord will do it.

Wait just a minute! In what context did Paul assure the Philippians of God's willingness to supply all their needs? Paul had just received their liberal gifts and tithes. The Philippians had done what was required of them; they had met God's condition. Have you? Perhaps the guidance you needed that morning was from Proverbs 3:9-10: "Honor the Lord from your wealth, and from the first of all your produce; so your barns will be filled with plenty, and your vats will overflow with new wine."

Some people read the most amazing things *into* the Scriptures. I remember hearing about a boy who wanted to marry a girl named Grace. He prayed God would show him if she was the right one. He opened his Bible to Philippians 1:2 and read, "*Grace* to you and peace from God our Father and the Lord Jesus Christ." What a flimsy foundation for guidance to enter into the implications of lifelong marriage.

My illustration of past experience has taught me not to rush ahead of God and buy a new car out of season. However, there came a time when I was in real need of a means of transportation. I prayed, "Lord only when it is Your perfect timing do I want a car. Even then You will have to find it for me and make all the circumstances fall into place."

That morning I read in my Bible, "Delight yourself in the Lord; and He will give you the desires of your heart" (Ps. 37:4). Now the Lord knew that one of the desires of my heart was for a better car, so I said, "Thank You Lord; I'll just delight myself in You and not worry about the rest."

Later, that same day, while I was driving down the road; I spotted a neat little car with a for sale sign sitting in the lot next to a service station. I felt a tugging in my spirit. The clear impression was: "That's the one!"

Quickly, I pulled over and asked the man to let me look at the car. A quiet sense of peace in my spirit told me this car was for me.

"All right, Lord," I said, a little excited. "I see two signs, Your Word this morning and now Your Holy Spirit seems to be telling me to buy this car, but I'm going to wait until the circumstances line up. You'll have to sell my old car before I can buy this one."

By now there was an increased sense of excitement. Two lights had lined up, and I was waiting for the third. Upon arriving home, I called a friend on the phone, and he bought my old car for cash. My confidence soared, because that was the third harbor light.

The car was a joy, and by the time I had put an additional 50,000 miles on it; it had cost me only forty dollars in repairs. This was a totally different experience to the one I bought outside of God's will, which cost me a small fortune in repair bills.

When the three harbor lights of guidance line up, God is making His will evident. We can rely on this principle. God's guidance is not usually a shadowy, haphazard thing. When the three witnesses come into one clear testimony, guidance can be increasingly clear. There are times, however, when these three witnesses become complicated, confused, or refuse to come together. This we will discuss in a later chapter.

CHAPTER
8
ABIDING IN THE WORD!

The Spectacular

In the days of Moses, God led His children through the desert by some pretty spectacular means. There was the pillar of smoke by day, fire by night, and the voice of God thundering to Moses on the mountain. Do you think that if we get to be spiritual enough, this will happen to us as well? No, that is highly unlikely.

The Exception or the Norm

Let us nail something down very firmly. It is my personal conviction that some 80% of our guidance comes through the Scriptures, approximately 15% comes through the Holy Spirit, and the last 5% may come through more unusual forms of guidance like dreams, visions, prophecy, or other more direct signs. *It is when we make the exception to be the norm that difficulties arise.* Attempts to coerce God or trick Him into personally desired forms of guidance is a dangerous game.

Jesus was quite specific in His instructions to those who believe on Him: "If you abide in My Word - hold fast to My teachings and live in accordance with them - you are truly My disciples" (John 8:31 Amplified).

No team of scientists in their right mind would attempt to construct a rocket and send it to the moon without thoroughly acquainting themselves with all the available data on rocket building and space travel. No team of doctors would undertake open-heart surgery without being thoroughly acquainted with all available knowledge and skill in that area.

Studying the Bible is a lifetime project. In fact, the more mature we become as Christians, the more we *need* to study it. Yet there are some Christians who either feel they have "arrived" or admit they are too busy doing "God's work" and say they do not need to read it. We must know and understand, to a measurable degree, the basic ground plan of God's Word. The Bible is the key to our knowledge of the character and nature of God as well as the key to understanding our own character and nature. It is the first of the three harbor lights of God's guidance.

How Does the Scripture Guide?

"Every Scripture is God-breathed - given by His inspiration - and profitable for instruction, for reproof and conviction of sin, for correction of error and discipline in obedience, and for training in righteousness [that is, in holy living, in conformity to God's will in thought, purpose and action], so that the man of God may be complete and proficient, well-fitted and thoroughly equipped for every good work" (II Tim. 3:16-17 Amplified).

There will always be areas in daily life where we are uncertain or unsure what to do or what God wants of us. However, if we knew His written Word, which is a declaration of His will and desire, and if we allowed His Word to become part of our flesh, deeply rooted in our being, we would *know* what to do in many areas where we now vacillate. Knowledge of God's will and desire to follow it is the cure to much spiritual confusion.

The Place of Integrity

There is an interesting comment on this in Proverbs 11:3: "The *integrity of the upright* will guide them, but the falseness of the treacherous will destroy them." Webster defines "integrity" as an unimpaired condition; soundness; firm adherence to a code of especially moral or artistic values; incorruptibility; the quality or state of being complete or undivided; completeness.

It is interesting that integrity is a state of *being complete* just as we read in II Timothy. If we allow the Scriptures to instruct us, convict of us sin, correct us, discipline us, and train us in righteousness, we will *become complete.* Integrity is impossible to achieve, however, without knowing and obeying the principles of the Word of God.

The Scripture guides in that it reproves from wrongdoing. It tells us how to dress, where to go, and where not to go. I do not have to stand outside a theater that is showing a pornographic film and ask, "Lord, should I go in or not?" It is perfectly clear in the Bible that I should not.

May I sound a word of warning here? The person who prays for guidance when he *already knows* the answer, opens himself up for deception! Suppose I find a wallet on the bus seat beside me. Inside there is $750 in cold cash. Should I pray, "Jesus, is it Your will that I keep this money - or should

I return it?" The very fact that I had to ask such a question indicates a propensity to be deceived. It follows that it is possible to receive an impression or hear a "voice" that urges me to keep it.

Merry's Notes

A delightful young couple got in trouble this way. They asked for guidance when they already knew the answer. John and Merry were very much in love. Both were Christians, filled with the Spirit, and they desired to serve God together. They were going to be married but had not set the date yet. Almost predictably, they were alone in her apartment one day and were overcome by their passion for each other. They got to their knees in the bedroom and prayed, "Lord, if it is Your will that we make love now before we're married, keep anybody from knocking on the door this afternoon. If it is against Your will that we do this, Lord, please send somebody to knock on the door right now, and we will take that as a sign." Of course nobody came to the door, and the young couple went ahead with their lovemaking. Later they experienced much depression and confusion and just could not understand why. After all, they had asked God to stop them if He did not want them to have sex. It was God's fault, not theirs.

When we pray for something God has already forbidden in His written Word, we open ourselves to receive guidance from the wrong source.

There are many Christian married people who have been led into adulterous situations in much the same way. They were so blinded by their love and hunger for companionship, they *claimed* they had asked God's guidance every step of the way. Plain meaning of Scripture helps us to understand that they must have listened to a wrong voice. God's Word is very plain, and He does not change His principles. Adultery is wrong and God would never, never lead you to sin (Jam. 1:13).

"He's the One!"

A young lady prayed for the Lord to show her whom she was to marry. One day in church she looked up at her pastor who was preaching and heard a little voice saying, "He's the one!" She responded with gratitude. She accepted that guidance and began her program of accomplishment. Had she known and obeyed the Bible, she would have rejected that little voice, because the pastor was already married. Yet for several years that young lady considered herself "spiritually engaged" and suffered increasing agonies over her "love." She finally came to a Christian counselor for help, but even then refused to acknowledge that her first "revelation" could be false. She was convinced that the love she felt for her married pastor was given to her by God, even though it was ripping her apart emotionally. Had she known that the wisdom that comes from above is first pure, peaceable, gentle, and reasonable (Jam. 3:17), she could have evaluated her guidance accordingly, saving herself, her pastor, and his family immeasurable pain.

When we pray for guidance over things like, "Should we sleep together now?" "Should I keep that wallet, Lord?" - we open ourselves to deception. To pray over such things or even to weigh them in your mind invites trouble.

When false guidance like that comes, we have the Scripture to correct us. Prayer or rationalization is unnecessary because we *know* from the Bible that we are not supposed to covet our friend's husband or steal our neighbor's wallet. Praying for guidance when we already know the answer is like a burglar who prays, "Lord, if You want me to pull that holdup in the bank, keep the police away. If You don't want me to steal, let a police car come by right now."

Balaam's Problem

In the book of Numbers there is a fascinating story about a prophet who prayed for guidance when he already knew what God wanted him to do. The Moabites and Midianites asked Balaam, the prophet, to curse the Israelites. When Balaam sought God's will, he was told not to curse the Israelites. A second time the Moabites and Midianites came to Balaam. This time they offered him many riches if he would curse the Israelites. Thinking about all that money (and how it could be used for the kingdom's work), Balaam asked God for advice again. This time God said, "Go with them, but speak only as I give you words."

Delighted over his new guidance, Balaam went. However, God sent an angel to stand in his way with a drawn sword. Balaam was riding on a donkey, and even though the angel was invisible to Balaam, the donkey could see him standing before him in the road. When the donkey refused to go on, Balaam became very angry. He struck the animal, and this is when the donkey opened its mouth and God spoke through the animal.

Balaam's end was a sad one. He became a false prophet who led many astray and was finally slain by the Israelites (Num. 22-24).

The books of Peter, Jude, and Revelation all warn against falling into error and false doctrine. "The integrity of the upright will guide them . . ." (Prov. 11:3).

Basics First

The Bible is full of examples of this kind of guidance. In II Samuel 24 we find King David coming to Araunah asking to buy his threshing place. God had told David through the prophet Gad to *buy* the place and build an altar there. Araunah offered to *give* David the threshing floor with oxen for burnt sacrifice and the threshing instruments for wood. But David had learned a lesson. Earlier in the chapter it is recorded how David had sinned, repented, and God had given him three choices of how his sin might be paid for, "Shall seven years of famine come to you in your land? Or will you flee three months before your foes while they pursue you? Or shall there be three days' pestilence in your land?" David chose not to become the prey of his enemies, and so God sent pestilence on the land and seventy thousand men died.

By now David saw his selfishness in allowing the innocent to die for his own sins. He cried out to God, "Behold, it is I who have sinned, and it is I who have done wrong; but these sheep, what have they done? Please let Thy hand be against me and against my father's house" (II Sam. 24:17).

No longer does David want another to pay for his sins or his sacrifices. Guided by his *new sense of integrity,* he says to Araunah, "No, but I will surely buy it from you for a price, for I will not offer burnt offerings to the Lord my God which cost me nothing" (vs. 24).

Integrity was also the guide for Abram who refused to take any spoils of war for himself. The story is found in Genesis 14. The cities of Sodom and Gomorrah had been taken captive by the enemy. Captured along with them was Lot and all his possessions. When Abram heard that his nephew had been taken away captive, he armed his 318 servants and went after the enemy. He defeated them in battle and brought back all the goods and the people, including Lot.

The high priest and king of Salem (later Jerusalem), Melchizedek, brought Abram bread and wine and blessed him, saying, "Blessed be Abram of God Most High, possessor of heaven and earth; and blessed be God Most High, Who has delivered your enemies into your hand" (vs. 19-20). Abram gave Melchizedek a tenth of everything he had brought back from the battle. The king of Sodom then asked Abram to release to him the persons he had rescued from the enemy kings. In return, he would let Abram keep all the goods for himself. But Abram *refused,* saying, "I have sworn to the Lord God Most High, possessor of heaven and earth, that I will not take a thread or a sandal thong or anything that is yours, lest you should say, 'I have made Abram rich'" (vs. 22-23).

The *integrity* of Abram caused him to recognize that God had won the battles against the enemy. Abram could not have done it on his own. Also, he saw that God alone is the source of his riches, not the king of Sodom. We all know the end of the story for Sodom. Because of the great wickedness of the people, God destroyed the city. Now if you or I had been in Abram's shoes, what would we have done? After all, didn't he risk his life and limb and all his trained servants to rescue the captives and the goods from the enemy? If that wicked king of Sodom wanted to give him some gold, silver, cattle, and goods as a token of his gratitude, what harm would there be in taking it? Abram was dwelling in the poor hill-country and the king of Sodom had plenty of fertile land in the valley. He could well afford to part with some of his goods.

The integrity of Abram was his guide. He took only what God gave him, lest a man should brag and say, "I made Abram rich." God had promised Abram riches, and Abram did not want anyone to doubt the source. He wanted to be able to say with a clear conscience, "the Lord has blessed me and kept His promises unto me."

Boaz was another who was guided by *integrity* in a tricky situation. Remember how Ruth came to glean grain in his field? Ruth was a young widow and her widowed mother-in-law told her that Boaz was a near kinsman of Ruth's deceased husband. According to Jewish law and custom, it was the duty and legal right of a man to marry the widow of his deceased brother - making sure she would have a child to carry on the deceased brother's name. This duty extended to the next kinsman in line if the first one refused.

Boaz had seen Ruth in the field and was attracted to her. Thus, on her mother-in-law's advice, she went to the threshing floor where Boaz was sleeping. She lay down at his feet. Startled, Boaz awoke.

"Who is there?" he cried out.

Shyly, Ruth told him who she was and that she had come to him because he was a near kinsman.

Boaz knew that Ruth was a virtuous woman who had come to him in good faith. He was pleased, for he had already fallen in love with her the first time he saw her - which really complicated matters in his mind. But Boaz also knew that there was another man in the city who was an even closer kinsman to Ruth than himself. This man had the *legal* right ahead of Boaz to take Ruth as his wife.

It was a tight spot for anyone. Ruth was there, waiting for him to take her as his wife. He had already fallen in love with her. No one would ever know the difference. Besides, she was a Gentile and no Jew would want her - or so he hoped. *Yet Boaz was guided by his integrity.* He knew the law and told Ruth that first he must go to this other man and inform him of his rights. If he did not want to exercise them, then Boaz could take Ruth as his wife.

Ruth lay at his feet until morning and slipped away before anyone could see that she had been there. Boaz went to see the other man who turned down his rights to marry Ruth, leaving Boaz free to claim her as his own. They eventually had a son named Obed who had a son named Jesse who was the father of David (Ruth 4:22).

Integrity guided Joseph in Egypt when he was overseer in the house of the captain of the guard. Potiphar had trusted everything he owned into the hands of Joseph whom he had bought as a slave. But when Potiphar's wife came after Joseph and asked him to go to bed with her, he turned her down.

"Your husband has trusted everything he owns to me," he said. "How can I do this great wickedness and sin against God?"

Scorned, Potiphar's wife accused Joseph of sexually accosting her, and he wound up in a prison dungeon. But that is where he met Pharaoh's chief butler who later told Pharaoh that Joseph could interpret dreams. When Joseph interpreted Pharaoh's dreams about the seven rich years and the seven years of famine to follow, Pharaoh made him ruler over all of Egypt. Joseph could have worked ten lifetimes trying to climb the social ladder in Egypt and never gained what those few years in prison brought him. Such is the reward of integrity (Gen. 39-41).

Personal integrity was the guide for these men of God in the Bible. And their integrity was based on a thorough knowledge of God's will as well as His character as it is revealed in His written Word. *Personal integrity, based on an intimate knowledge of the Word of God, is our most basic avenue of guidance.* All other guidance goes on from there, but without this foundation we can never fully enter into God's perfect will and plan for our individual or corporate lives.

CHAPTER
9
THE HOLY SPIRIT SPEAKS

How? Audible Voice?

The second of the three harbor lights of guidance is *the inner witness of the Holy Spirit.* In the book of Acts we find many examples of this. One example appears in Acts 8:29: "And the Spirit said to Philip, 'Go up and join this chariot.'"

My question is, how did the Holy Spirit speak to Philip? Was it an audible voice? Was it something within Philip's spirit? We are not told exactly how the Spirit spoke; yet Philip knew the words and obeyed them.

Scholarly, Bible-believing men whom I trust, have heard God speak in an audible voice. Such was the experience of young Samuel with Eli in the Temple (I Sam. 3:10). Although I have never heard God speak in an audible voice, I have heard Him speak distinct words deep inside me.

In Columbia, South America, I was lying in bed when the presence of the Lord came into the room and the Holy Spirit said very distinctly, "I want you to go back to school!"

It could not have been clearer if my wife had spoken the words right next to me. It was spoken straight and strong and right into my spirit. It was not a demanding, urgent voice. If it had been, I would immediately have suspected the source to be someone or something other than the Lord.

The vocal impression was warm, but firm. I knew it was the Lord.

In Chapter 1 we discussed James's characteristics of wisdom coming from God contrasted with the wisdom coming from below. The wisdom from above is always *peaceable* and *pure*. When God speaks, there is always a sense of peace deep within our spirit, even if we do not like what He is saying.

Arguing With the Umpire

I did not like it when the Lord told me to go back to school. I had already graduated from one Bible college. I had a wife and children to support, and I argued with the Holy Spirit. Three days later, however, there were further instructions: "I want you to go to the Reformed Episcopal Seminary in Philadelphia, Pennsylvania."

It did not seem logical for a Spirit-filled Bible teacher to go back to seminary, but the voice that spoke to my spirit was indeed the voice of God. He did not speak to my mind, emotions, or will. Rather He spoke to my inner being - that part of me which is spirit alone. And so I said, "Lord, I'm willing, now arrange the circumstances."

He did, and I went. Many times over the years I have seen the fruit of that obedience.

Recognizing His Voice

The Holy Spirit can and does speak sometimes in distinct, understandable words. On occasion this may be external and audible, but this is the exception. Most often it is internal and subjective, but perfectly clear and distinct.

Receiving guidance depends greatly on our ability to recognize the voice of God when He speaks to us. It was important for Philip to recognize and obey when the Holy Spirit spoke to him. It is important that we do the same.

Equipment

Our textbook for this kind of direct guidance is the book of Acts. Here we find countless examples of the Holy Spirit giving specific instructions to the disciples, i.e., "Go here and do this." Earlier, Jesus Himself had told the disciples what to do. Jesus told His disciples that He would soon go to the Father, but that they should not grieve, "I assure you that it is a good thing for you that I should go away. For if I did not go away, the divine helper would not come to you. But if I go, then I will send him to you. . . . He will guide you into everything that is true" (John 16:7,13 Phillips).

After Jesus' resurrection, He showed Himself to the disciples, and before His ascension, He emphasized that they were to stay in Jerusalem and wait for the fulfillment of the promise: "Before many days are passed you will be baptized with the Holy Spirit . . . you are to be given power when the Holy Spirit has come to you" (Acts 1:5,8 Phillips).

Learning a Skill

At Pentecost, tongues of fire descended from heaven and the assembled followers of Jesus Christ were baptized in the Holy Spirit, just as He had promised. This introduced the disciples into a brand-new realm of experiencing the presence and power of God. It also opened them to the influence of other spiritual powers, and in reading the book of Acts, we see how the disciples had to learn the skill of knowing the voice of God, sometimes by trial and error.

In our lives, the baptism in the Holy Spirit opens the door for us to receive God's power. It is our tool-kit, but we must learn to use it. It is like learning to play the piano or use a computer. At first you hunt and peck, thinking you will never catch on. A sense of failure or inability nags you until you pass a certain point at which time faith kicks in and you realize that you really will be able to learn.

On several occasions I have followed what I thought was the leading of the Holy Spirit only to find myself in a blind alley.

"Go down this street, there is a brick house on the right. Go there, the man needs Jesus." I drive down the street but there is no brick house! However, I am learning! And at least I am willing to be obedient. We should be encouraged by the fact that the disciples did not *always* recognize the leading of God either.

Restraint

Often we find that the Holy Spirit *restrains* us from a certain action. This would not be necessary if we went in the right direction in the first place. The apostles, being human, had the same experiences. Paul and Silas were on their way through Phrygia and Galatia, "but the *Holy Spirit* prevented them from speaking God's message in Asia" (Acts 16:6-7 Phillips).

It seems strange that the Holy Spirit would ever forbid anyone to preach the Good News. We are told to preach the Word to everyone, everywhere, right? No, there is a time to speak and a time to refrain from speaking. This is especially good advice for people who try to cram religion down everybody's throat.

"But I felt led to stand on the street corner and preach about Jesus Christ," one man told me. "I ask everybody who comes by if they know Jesus as their Savior."

That's good IF the Holy Spirit commissioned you to do it. But, learning if you are down there on the corner because you have a strong urge inside you, no peace, and you have got to do something to satisfy your restlessness, then it is not the Holy Spirit's direction. It is simply your own undisciplined human spirit. Such "ministry" does incalculable harm to the spreading of the Gospel. God knows the perfect timing. He knows when hearts and minds are tender and ready to receive His Word. When *He* sends you, people listen and a harvest is reaped.

A few years back there was a visitation of the Holy Spirit in a Midwestern town. During a meeting the Holy Spirit fell on the congregation. The visitation spread through the city, and every day the minister of the church and the evangelist went to visit people in their homes or places of business. They drove down the street praying, praising the Lord, and waiting for the gentle tugging of the Holy Spirit who said, "Stop at *this* gas station, go in *here* for a cup of coffee, drive into *that* car lot, speak to *that* man. . . ."

Every single person they spoke to received salvation through Jesus Christ as his Savior. Most of us, however, are so dense that God has to start leading us through *negative* or *restrictive* guidance.

"Don't speak the word in Asia!"

When Paul and Silas came to Mysia they tried to enter Bithynia, "but again the Holy Spirit would not permit them." They still did not know where God wanted them to go. They wanted to get at the teeming millions in Asia, but God said, "*No.*" He was leading them by restrictive guidance.

I once thought that Paul, Silas, and the other apostles wore halos over their heads. Like you, I thought they were able to discern instantly what God wanted them to do. I was glad when I discovered in practice that this was not the case.

In Bible college I had a professor whom I respected greatly. Once in class he told us, "This morning I got up to pray and fell asleep!" Spontaneously I cheered out loud. Everybody in the class turned to look at me. The professor grinned and said, "What's the matter, Mr. Mumford? Are you glad to find out that I'm human?"

Embarrassed, I confessed, "To tell you the truth, sir, I am. I sometimes fall asleep during my morning prayer time, but I didn't think anybody else did."

When I first started listening to the prompting of the voice within, I often went in the wrong direction, but I was not aware that anybody else did. I was relieved when I discovered that Paul and Silas and the other apostles had the same problem. So do our present-day spiritual "giants!"

Trial and Error

Remember the occasion when the disciples crossed the Sea of Galilee and Jesus said, "Beware of the leaven of the Pharisees?"

Reasoning among themselves as to what He meant, one of the disciples said, "He must have forgotten the lunch." This, of course, had nothing to do with what Jesus was talking about. Their inability to perceive is comforting to me in two ways. One, it shows that all good disciples are a little slow to catch on, and two, that the Master is always rich in patience as He teaches us His ways. In fact, it is because of our spiritual density that God is forced to use more dramatic forms of guidance (visions) to impress His will upon us.

What would have happened if Paul had persisted in going into Asia? Possibly, the whole course of history could have been changed by this one man's failure to follow his guidance. Paul was not able to discern *where* God wanted him to go, but he did know God wanted him to go somewhere. He probably reasoned, "There is a real need in Asia, I think I will go there." How did the Holy Spirit restrain him? It may have been by an audible voice, but more likely it was by upsetting Paul's peace. He tried preaching in Asia, but suddenly the internal peace of God was upset, and he knew he was on the wrong track. This trial-and-error method continued until Paul was finally in a position to hear the positive guidance of the Holy Spirit.

Get It Moving

There are people who sit still waiting for God to speak. "God, if You want me to go to church this Sunday, speak to me." But God wants us on the move. It is very difficult to turn the steering wheel of a stopped car. Get it moving and you can turn the wheel easily. Likewise, you can turn the helm of a docked ship, but nothing happens. It is only when the ship is on the move that it responds to the helmsman's touch on the wheel.

Sanctified Intellect

If I cannot seem to get any direct guidance from God about where I am to go or what I am to do next, I use my best judgment, my *sanctified intellect*, and get moving. I have already surrendered my will to God and asked Him to lead me or restrict me if I am heading the wrong way. I keep my inward ear listening for the prompting of the Spirit, and as I go I let Him guide.

Several years ago we moved to a new city and started a search for a church in which to worship. The Lord had not given any direct guidance. We visited one church, but there was no peace. Then another, still no peace. Finally, a third and the peace of God began flowing like a river.

I could have given up after the first two tries and said, "Lord, I tried two churches and You didn't tell me anything so I'm just going to sit here and wait until You let me know where to go." It is not that there was anything wrong with the first two churches, but God had a specific plan and place for us, as He does for each one. But you have to keep trying until you find it.

Principles not Methods

A young man who graduated from Bible college with me, showed great promise in school. He was married, had three children, and was living in one of the small cottages provided for married students. A couple of months after graduation I went to see him.

"What are your plans?" I asked.

He said, "Well, since I do not have any leadings from the Lord, I am just going to stay right here until Jesus tells me what to do." And there he sat until the "unspiritual" faculty helped him move out to give room for another family just starting school.

"What should he have done?" you ask. Even without *specific* leading he could have used his sanctified intellect and at least begun to *move*.

"I'll find a home for my family and start traveling as an evangelist." If he received negative guidance from the Lord, he could have changed directions. "I'll find employment and at least assume the responsibility of providing for my family." That is one thing he could be sure God wanted him to do. If you walk in the little light you have, God will always supply more light.

As long as you move with a sincere desire to do God's will, He will guide you into the right place. But if you sit still and try to sweat God out, you will find that He will not yield. I have tried it!

God will not be manipulated, and it is useless to try to figure Him out. *Guidance involves principles to be learned - not techniques to be mastered.*

I once knew a fellow who wanted to learn all about healings. He studied every incident of healing in the New Testament. He thought that by figuring out the *technique* Jesus and the disciples used, he would tap the secret of their power. Much to his dismay he discovered there were not two healings alike. The only common denominator was dependence upon the Father - which, incidentally, was the secret of the power of our Lord Jesus Christ.

Guidance is like that. Learning to discern the voice of God is a skill, and it can be learned, but there are no two circumstances alike.

God Leads, Satan Pushes

When the Holy Spirit speaks, He may speak in positive guidance, or He may use negative guidance. And negative guidance, which often manifests itself by the disruption of inner peace, may be preventive guidance to keep us away from harm which we will never know about unless we fail to heed the guidance.

While I was Dean of a Bible college in New York, my wife and I started on a trip to Delaware to interview some prospective students. We had not planned the trip or prayed about it. The farther we drove down the freeway, the more upset we became deep inside.

"Lord, what's the matter?" I asked.

Inside I felt the response, "You had better stop right now."

I said to my wife, "Honey, do you sense something wrong?"

She said, "I sense God's big hand in front of us saying, 'Stop.'" I put on the brakes and pulled over to the side of the road.

"Let's just stop and see what happens," I said. As soon as we stopped the car, the unrest and heaviness lifted. I said, "Thank You, Jesus," and turned the car around.

When we started back in the other direction, the glory of the Lord filled that car, and we began to worship Him. What we had been heading for only God knows. But whatever it was, God's negative guidance had disquieted our peace and warned us not to go farther. It is important that we learn to recognize the restraining hand of God.

Sometimes we wonder if the negative guidance could be Satan's method of keeping us from doing God's will. Remember, though, that Satan cannot imitate the peace of God. When that peace is disturbed, take care.

We may hear an inner voice saying, "You are not praying enough. You need to pray more." Surely, Satan would not tell you to pray! Sure he would. There are two ways Satan can trap us. Either by leading us into obvious worldly sin or by pushing us overboard on some spiritual tangent. Sometimes God wants us to act - not pray. Satan can also quote Scripture, talk about spiritual things, and impress upon us great religious fervor.

I counseled a lady who had come under counterfeit spiritual pressure. Voices were telling her to fast and pray, deprive herself of sleep, wear long black dresses, never read the newspaper, or listen to musical instruments. She was under great duress, and she was forced to take another look and see that even "spiritual" guidance can come from Satan.

One way we can tell the difference between the voice of God and a counterfeit is the sense of *peace*. The voice which speaks peace is of God; the voice which speaks urgency is either of Satan or comes from your own human nature. *God leads; Satan pushes.*

The demanding voice says, "Quit your job right now. Don't wait for tomorrow. You are disobedient if you don't!" If we follow such advice, we are in trouble, because God seldom speaks like that except in emergencies.

Mountains and Valleys

The Greek word for god is *theos*. This is the same root that our word "enthusiasm" comes from. The ancient Greeks looked at someone who was *entheos* as someone who was possessed by a god and transported into ecstasy. We need to recognize the fine line between genuine, spiritual enthusiasm (which like deep water in a river may run fast but without froth and foam) and a kind of demonizing that leads us to frantically play the role of a religious cheerleader without any inner peace. As far as I am concerned, enthusiasm in religious realms can be a symptom of spiritual disease. Such things as excessive political action, single-issue churches and leadership, faith healing, finances, or an over-emphasis on social action, i.e. making the Church and the kingdom to appear money-centered, can take the place of genuine biblical vision and spiritual motivation. Building programs and personalities are not an adequate substitute for the presence of God to keep God's people "enthusiastic" about "religious things." Mountain peaks of enthusiasm can be just as dangerous as deep valleys in our walk with God.

When we come to know the abiding peace of God deep in our spirit, we have reached a balance and a stability that cannot be upset by circumstances or urgent voices speaking to our mind or emotions. Nor can we be fooled by counterfeit guidance, because we have learned to recognize the voice of God. Receiving genuine guidance involves learning certain principles.

There are multitudes of people who have come into a relationship with Jesus Christ and been baptized in the Holy Spirit, but they go through life without practicing and developing the skill of following God's daily leading. They are like one who receives a beautiful concert piano as a gift, but is satisfied to play with only one finger.

The baptism in the Holy Spirit potentially brings with it the promise of divine guidance, but we must understand the need for practice and development in receiving it. The author of Hebrews writes, "At a time when you should be teaching others, you need teachers yourselves to repeat to you the ABC of God's revelation to men. You have become people who need a milk diet and cannot face solid food! For anyone who continues to live on 'milk' is obviously immature - he simply has not grown up. 'Solid food' is only for the adult, that is, for the man *who has developed by experience* his power to discriminate between what is good and what is bad for him" (Heb. 5:12-14 Phillips).

The only way to develop the ability to discriminate between the voice of God and other voices is by *experience* and by use. There are many voices clamoring for our attention. It is important now, more than ever before in history, that we learn to know the voice of God.

CHAPTER
10
THE PEACE OF GOD

We have mentioned the activity of the Holy Spirit as the subjective witness speaking to our spiritual man. This voice is the active function of the Holy Spirit. The second function, equally as important, is the passive aspect of the ministry of the Holy Spirit known as the "Peace of God."

Few words are as abused and misunderstood today as PEACE. We see it painted on signs and fences; riots and protest marches are carried on under its banner; bumper-stickers read WORLD PEACE NOW. Even the peace sign repeatedly comes back into vogue. (Incidentally, that upside-down broken cross within a circle was designed in the first century during witches' masses to signify the power of Satan over the broken power of Jesus Christ).

God's Umpire

The peace of God in guidance functions according to the principle outlined in Colossians 3:15, "And let the peace (soul harmony which comes) from the Christ rule (act as umpire continually) in your hearts - deciding and settling with finality all questions that arise in your minds - [in that peaceful state] to which [as members of Christ's] one body you were also called [to live]" (Amplified Bible).

This means that the peace of God is to act as umpire within us for or against an intended course of action. This is an important aspect of any subjective guidance.

How does the peace of God do this? It occurs when we have conscious rest or assurance in our heart concerning a matter. Otherwise we have unrest, uncertainty, or agitation.

We know better than to argue with an umpire in a ball game. He has the last word. Either we are safe, or we are out. To argue with the umpire may get us thrown out of the game. The peace of God is the umpire who calls the strikes and causes us to know whether we are on safe ground or in error. What is the nature of this peace? How do we know when we have it? Are there conditions for having it?

Absence of Disturbance

Unless we meet certain conditions, we cannot know the peace of God, and consequently, we are in great danger of missing God's guidance for our lives.

The peace of God is not a mere absence of disturbance around us.

"Oh, it's these miserable circumstances around us," we complain. "The rent is due, the children are sick, and the neighbors are nasty. My boss is grumpy and somebody stole the hubcaps off my car. No wonder I do not have any peace."

The ones who march for peace say, "Oh, if we could just have another government, end all wars, find a cure for AIDS, and ban everything that causes pollution, then we would have peace."

Peace Defined

But the peace of God is *not* dependent upon circumstances. It is a state of being that originates within us. We are conscious of being at rest and peace, regardless of the circumstances around us.

Jesus was in the boat with the disciples in the middle of the Sea of Galilee when a storm blew up (Matt. 8:23). The waves were bursting over the sides and the disciples were frightened, but Jesus was sleeping soundly in the back of the boat.

"Master, Master, don't You care that we perish?" they shouted as they woke Him.

Jesus said, "Everything is all right."

"But Lord, You do not understand the circumstances - look at those waves!" the disciples cried.

Confidently, He arose and spoke to the waves. He had the peace of God within. No waves, regardless of their size, could upset Him.

One day I was driving my car on an ice-covered road. Suddenly the car started sliding. I saw telephone poles and guard rails looming up ahead. Yet inside me was a real sense of peace telling me, "Everything is all right, Bob, do not panic. I have My hand on the wheel." And thank the Lord, He did. After two and a half spins, my car stopped facing the guard rail without a scratch.

His peace is more than coming home from work and finding everything quiet and calm, your family in perfect harmony. No, the peace of God can be with you even when you come home tired and find the children are fighting, the television going full blast, the bills are due, and the roof has a leak. His peace inside of you makes everything all right.

There is an old story of a group of artists who were asked to paint a picture of peace. Each chose a different scene. One painted a sunset, another a quiet ocean, and a third a harvest scene. But one painted a picture of a roaring waterfall; and just above the thundering water, he painted a little bird asleep on a slender branch, her head under her wing. Doesn't she hear the roaring fall just below? Sure, but the roar cannot touch her. She has wings.

The peace of God is a supernatural rest in the midst of surrounding unrest. To wait for circumstances to change so we can have peace could mean waiting forever. Circumstances will not really change until first we are changed.

In Philippians 4:6-7, Paul gives us a condition for this peace and also tells us something of its nature, "Do not worry over anything whatever; tell God every detail of your needs in earnest and thankful prayer, and the peace of God, which transcends human understanding, will keep constant guard over your hearts and minds as they rest in Christ Jesus" (Phillips). The peace of God *transcends* human understanding. We may question ourselves and our ability to remain peaceful in times of adversity. Our friends and neighbors may comment, "How can you be so peaceful when you just lost your job and your wife is in the hospital?" But that is what the peace of God does, transcending all understanding (and misunderstandings, I might add).

On Guard

The peace of God *guards* our hearts and minds as they rest in Christ Jesus; for it is in these areas (our emotions and intellect) that we are most susceptible to false guidance. When my emotions or intellect are upset, I know to be on my guard.

I was speeding down a country highway late one night when, without any explanation, my "peace within" was disturbed. Something in my mind began to go click . . . click . . . click. Something was wrong.

"What is it, Lord?" I asked. "My peace has been disturbed."

Softly, in my spirit, I sensed a warning: "Watch out for deer!" Having become accustomed to listening to the kind of guidance that comes from a disturbance of the peace within, I simply said, "Thank You, Lord," and slowed down.

Rounding the next bend, my headlights suddenly picked up the form of a large doe standing beside the road. Startled, she leaped right in front of the car. But since I had already been warned, I was able to stop in time without hitting her. I had been prepared by a form of guidance that is not often recognized.

The peace *of* God cannot be ours unless we have *made peace with God.* And peace with God can come only through our repentance and confession followed by God's forgiveness. For instance, if someone had committed adultery five years ago and in order to keep it hidden, had mentally suppressed it, it would be impossible for him to know peace *with* God. How could he know the peace of

God with something like that gnawing at him night and day?

If we confess our sins, God is just and will forgive us. That is a definite promise. However, we are required to open up all hidden sins, which is often a frightening experience. Yet how wonderful it is to have everything cleaned up between us and the Lord Jesus Christ.

Behavior and Attitudes

Our *behavior and attitudes* affect our peace with God. There is an admonition and warning to husbands in I Peter 3:7, "You husbands should try to understand the wives you live with, honoring them as physically weaker yet equally heirs with you of the grace of life. If you do not do this, you will find it impossible to pray properly" (Phillips). Peter's principle, of course, applies not only to husbands in their relationship with their wives, but to every other relationship as well. You cannot know the guidance or sense the leading of the Spirit when you have *turmoil* inside. Turmoil is like the tinfoil dropped by enemy planes - it jams our spiritual radar.

Many people who come to me for counseling and prayer are all worked up inside. Discovering this, I say, "All right, come out with it. I know there is something hidden in your life, an unsettled matter between you and God." Even if the disturbance is manifested by a bad relationship with another person, I know it is still caused by some short circuit with God. (Remember the difference between symptoms and causes?)

Loving His Commands

We cannot know the peace of God if we are *disobedient* to His law. Isaiah says, "If only you had paid attention to My commandments! Then your well-being would have been like a river, and your righteousness like the waves of the sea" (Isa. 48:18). Verse 22 reads, "'There is no peace for the wicked,' says the Lord."

Love is another condition for peace. The psalmist sings, "Those who love Thy law have great peace, and nothing causes them to stumble" (Ps. 119:165). If we are filled with God's Spirit, live in His Spirit, and walk in that Spirit, we are guaranteed the continuous presence of God's peace in our lives. "If you love Me," Jesus said, "keep My commandments . . ." (John. 14:21).

God's Tranquilizer

Peace with God will bring the peace of God until it settles your nerves, fills your mind, floods over your spirit, and in the midst of any uproar around you, gives you the assurance that everything is all right. You can have peace in the kitchen with pots boiling over and guests coming for dinner. It can be yours on the front lines of battle with guns going off over your head. You can claim it on the freeway with cars piling up on all sides, knowing you are going to be late for an important appointment. The peace of God guards your heart and mind, and you rest in Jesus Christ. People who know the peace of God do not take tranquilizers. He is their tranquilizer.

Imitations

Peace within is our key to this basic form of guidance. When you know the peace of God, you will find the leading of the Spirit quite accurate and very precise. Guidance coming as the peace of God literally arbitrates and settles the disputes in our hearts and minds concerning specific actions.

Can you depend on an inner *voice* alone to settle a matter in which you need guidance? In the midst of an argument with yourself you say, "Lord, You know I am willing to give my rent money to this urgent cause if that is what You desire." Suddenly there is the peace of God inside. No more churning, no more stirred-up feelings. "Sure, I will give my rent money. The Lord will provide."

A carpenter friend of mine received an urgent call from a missionary in South America. The mission needed someone to build a church structure. The carpenter was being asked to quit his job in the States and come down and help. There is good biblical authority for such a call. In fact, it was in answer to such a call that Paul left Asia and went to Macedonia. The carpenter had two of the harbor lights in line - the objective standard (God's Word) and the circumstances (divine providence). But the middle harbor light, the inner witness of the Holy spirit (the peace of God), was missing. He prayed, "Lord, I'm willing to go." But still there was no peace, just an urgent unrest inside.

Some people mistake that urgent unrest as a call from God. They are often led far astray, with tragic consequences. God may speak suddenly, causing a stirring in your spirit; but He very seldom requires you to do anything until you have recognized His peace and assurance about the matter.

In this particular case, the peace never did come, and the carpenter wisely concluded that God did not want him to go to South America. His refusal to go meant the church structure could not be built. Yet time proved he was right, for in less than a year an earthslide destroyed every existing building in that region. It was only then that the carpenter received the peace of God to go - and he went.

Another friend of mine was enroute to the Philippine Islands. He stopped in San Francisco to purchase a tape recorder. He was attracted to a machine costing $300. However, he had only $320 to spend for the entire trip. Inside he heard a voice say, "Buy that tape recorder."

"But Lord," he argued, "I can get a tape recorder for $50!" He walked around the store looking at cheaper models, but the guidance was too strong to dismiss. Returning to the expensive machine he said, "Lord, you know I am willing, but I have got to know this guidance is from You." Suddenly there was a peace within, and my friend purchased the expensive machine. Arriving in the Philippines he discovered that the electrical current in the Islands fluctuates. His new recorder had a built-in stabilizer. Had he bought a cheaper one, he would not have been able to use it.

The peace of God was the umpire, the deciding factor.

Unless you know *peace with God and the peace of God,* divine guidance can never become perfected in your life. Peace is the deciding factor, because *it is the one thing Satan cannot imitate or counterfeit.* Satan can imitate the voice of

God.   He can speak through prophecy, signs, visions, dreams and revelations. He can even counterfeit love and goodness and appear as an angel of light. But he *cannot* imitate the peace of God.

Peace to This House

When Jesus sent His twelve disciples out to preach the gospel, He gave them authority to expel evil spirits and heal all kinds of diseases. He also gave them some sound advice, "Wherever you go . . . find out someone who is respected, and stay with him until you leave. As you enter his house give it your blessing. If the house deserves it, the peace of your blessing will come to it.. But if it does not, your peace will return to you" (Matt. 10:11-13 Phillips).

Jesus told His disciples to greet a house upon entering. Almost every one of the letter writers in the New Testament followed this advice, even in their writing, as they started with the greeting, "May grace and peace be unto you from God the Father and His Son, Jesus Christ."

This was not a mere formality. When Jesus walked into a room He said, "Peace be unto you," and I do not think He was merely being polite. Something happened in a room when He spoke those words, something of the same nature as when He spoke and the stormy waters were calmed. Nervous minds and hearts were calmed at His words.

I have gone into homes and in the name of Jesus said, "Peace be unto you," and immediately sensed something was wrong. That little clicker inside me went off. I would look around - a picture of Jesus was hanging on the wall, Bibles were here and there.   It looked like a spiritual household. But inside me the Umpire was saying, "Watch out! Be careful! Walk softly! There is something in this house that is not receptive to the peace of God."

Once, driving down the highway, I was listening to a radio preacher, "You need to know Jesus. Salvation is in following Jesus," he said. It sounded good, but inside me the internal warning signal went off. Click . . . click . . . click. "Watch out, something is wrong," it said. I argued with the Umpire, "I'll just hear this man out; he sounds good enough." But at the end of the program the announcer revealed that the program originated from a source which denies the deity of Christ. The words had sounded good enough, but the Umpire within had warned. That man was not speaking truth because he represented a group which did not believe the whole counsel of God.

The peace of God is the umpire within us, guarding us against slipping into wrong action or false doctrines.

CHAPTER
11
SURROUNDED BY
CIRCUMSTANCES!

Under the Circumstances

Our outward lives are a continuous unfolding of circumstances, and most of us have particular ways of interpreting them. If the Dow-Jones index is up and we make $5000 on the stock market we say, "God is making everything work out right for me." But if the roof leaks, the car breaks down, or we lose our last penny in the stock market, we might say, "Under the circumstances I guess I am all right, but life sure is giving me a hard time."

In reply to this, one might ask, "What are you doing *under* the circumstances?" Paul says in Romans, "All who will take God's gift of forgiveness and approval are kings of life" (Rom. 5:17 Living Letters). We are designed to live above the circumstances.

We have already discussed how God uses circumstances to guide us whether we are aware of it or not, and how He allows adverse circumstances to crowd us back into His will. Once we have committed our lives to Christ, God is in complete control of every circumstance in our lives, good *and* bad. If Satan gets in a lick or two, it is only because God has allowed it, not because He is not looking. The Bible specifically promises that for those who love God, all things work together for good (Rom. 8:28). Mark it down that this refers to *all things.*

Remember the three harbor lights of guidance? They are: 1) the written Word of God (objective standard); 2) the Holy Spirit (subjective witness); and 3) circumstances (the providence of God). It is to this last light, God's use of circumstances in direct, conscious guidance that we now look.

Vulnerability

It is possible to read the Word of God out of context and therefore be misled. What we may understand to be the Holy Spirit speaking can be equally misleading; unless the peace of God is present and the leading conforms to the Word of God. Likewise, responding to circumstances apart from the other two can lead us even farther astray. The same circumstance can be misinterpreted in one of four basic ways according to our outlook on life:

1. "God is putting me through a test."
2. "I'm being punished for my disobedience."
3. "The devil is after me."
4. "I'm being persecuted for righteousness' sake."

Most of us are more easily swayed by circumstances than by anything else. After all, circumstances are visible and seem very real. Anything that touches us outwardly is circumstance, i.e. cold, heat, hunger, pain, etc. If we want to grow up into mature sons and daughters of God, guided by His Holy Spirit, we must allow God to break us of vulnerability to circumstances. We *can* learn to discern God's hand in circumstances in positive or negative guidance, but we must *also* learn that favorable or unfavorable circumstances *cannot be taken alone* as a sign that we are in or out of the will of God.

Favorable or Unfavorable

Recall the story in Numbers 22 concerning Balaam who was bribed to prophesy against the children of Israel. God set a series of circumstances into action to prevent Balaam from going against His will, i.e. the rebellious donkey, the narrow place where the donkey crushed Balaam's foot, and ultimately, the angel with the drawn sword who nearly killed Balaam.

Balaam was not looking for guidance. He *knew* he was going against God's will and refused to pay any attention. But God *did* arrange a set of negative circumstances to stop him. Spiritually, this principle is known as *divine resistance.* As a person or a group of persons insists on going their own way, God turns up His rheostat, resisting the people from going their own way, a way which would result in self-destruction.

The Holy Spirit had Hosea warn Israel that continued persistence in her own way would result in the increase of the intensity of God's corrective measures. It is important for us to know that God will arrange a set of negative circumstances to stop us when we are going against His will. The increase of the severity of the circumstances seems to be in proportion to the strength of our human determination and our continued rebellion.

Confirmation Necessary

An impulsive Christian young man when asked to do chores around the house would become upset, get in his car and drive downtown to witness for Christ on a street corner. He would tell his parents, "I'm going out to work for the Lord."

One day he prayed, "Lord, teach me to walk in Your will." Soon afterward, something happened at home to upset him, and he ran out to his car to go downtown "for the Lord." But the car would not start. There seemed to be nothing mechanically wrong, it just would not start. He finally gave up, went back in the house, and forced himself to remain calm.

That night as the family started out for church, he got into his car, turned the key in the ignition, and it started immediately. He was mystified. A few days later it happened again. The young man became upset at home, ran to the car, and it refused to start. Yet when the family went someplace later, the car started like a dream.

After three or four times the young man became suspicious. Once he went out in the morning just to test-start the car. It started right up and ran smoothly. Yet later that day, when he felt restless and wanted to go for a ride, it would not start at all. At last he prayed, "Lord, what is wrong with my car?"

The answer was clear: "You wanted to learn how to walk in My will? I have kept you from going your own way."

He could only say, "Thank You, Lord!"

God has the power to make your car stop or run. If you are not certain, whether you are moving in or out of His will, then pay attention to circumstances like that. It could be a flat tire, missing the plane at the airport, or a house you thought God wanted you to buy which was sold to someone else. If God had wanted you there on time or wanted you in that house, no circumstance could have prevented it from happening. So thank the Lord for *all* circumstances, and learn to look for and recognize His guiding hand.

Buying the Field

God also uses circumstances to *confirm* His guidance. The word of God came to Jeremiah and told him to buy some land. "Behold, Hanamel the son of Shallum your uncle is coming to you, saying, 'Buy for yourself my field which is at Anathoth, for you have the right of redemption to buy it.'" Reading on we find, "Then Hanamel my uncle's son came to me in the court of the guard according to the word of the Lord, and said to me, 'Buy my field, please, that is at Anathoth, which is in the land of Benjamin; for you have the right of possession and the redemption is yours; buy it for yourself.' *Then I knew that this was the word of the Lord.* I bought the field" (Jer. 32:7-9).

Here are two of the harbor lights of guidance lined up: God speaking directly to Jeremiah by His Spirit and in accordance with God's written Word (the reference to the right of one relative to buy or redeem land from another). From a natural, logical point of view, however, it still looked like a pretty ridiculous proposition. The prophet was a prisoner and the land he was told to buy was occupied by the army of Nebuchadnezzar who was holding Jerusalem under siege. But Jeremiah knew the outcome of the siege. He knew he and all his people would be taken as captives to Babylon. He also knew, however, that one day the land would be returned to the children of Judah.

Experience had taught Jeremiah that even when God spoke to him and the word was confirmed by the written law, he should not make a move or conclude that God Himself had spoken *until* he saw the circumstances fall into place. Once he *knew* this was guidance from God, he bought the field and did not worry about the army of occupation who happened to be camped there - nor about his own imprisonment and impending captivity.

Once we are sure our leading is from the Lord, it is time to drive down our stakes and not permit anything or anyone to lead us away. *Failure to obey clear guidance leads to compromise.* Once the three harbor lights line up, we must keep a straight course regardless of doubts or feelings.

Smoke Screen Ahead

During World War II, Navy destroyers operating in enemy waters were given definite compass headings by the group flagship. Under no circumstance were they to alter their course. Immediately afterward, a low-flying airplane spread a thick smoke screen just ahead of them. They plowed into the dense smoke, but the blinding circumstances did not deter the various captains because they had received clear instructions. If one of the captains had doubted the initial orders, begun to get nervous, and felt like he should change his course, he would have immediately endangered his own ship as well as others.

Once guidance is clearly given by the Lord, confirmed by witnesses, and established in your heart, you can expect a Satanic smoke screen of confusing voices and circumstances to surround your frail vessel. Remember, steady-as-she-goes, for the course has been set. As we sail on in faith and obedience to our initial guidance, *the end is guaranteed.* On the other side of the smoke screen is clear sunlight.

Initial Leadings

When you married, were you sure that the young lady or the young man was the one God wanted for you? Then hold to the initial leading, remembering even perfect marriages have their ups and downs in the smoke screens of life.

So, now you are in school and struggling with finances. Circumstances demand that you live in a tiny apartment, and each time you try to study, the baby cries. Every time you try to communicate, it ends in an argument, and you say, "It could not have been the Lord who brought us together. We are both so miserable."

Now if you were sure of your initial leading, then remember your marriage vows: In sickness or health, rich or poor, good or bad *circumstances.*

In the days preceding my graduation from college, I was becoming anxious over my direction in life. Most of my other classmates knew exactly what they were supposed to do, but I was still waiting for God to direct me. Even though I wanted to go to the mission field, there was an increasing awareness that the Holy Spirit was directing me toward the area of medicine. As the witness and peace grew within me, God directed me to Hebrew 10:5, which said, "Sacrifice and offering Thou hast not desired, but a body Thou hast prepared for me." This was the objective standard of my commitment to do the will of God. Two of the three harbor lights had fallen into place even though my desires were to go in a different direction.

Then, on the day of graduation, someone stuck a pamphlet in my hand promoting a medical school. I wanted to be a minister with all my heart, but now the third harbor light had fallen in line. I knew what I must do. Going home I fell on my knees.

"Lord," I prayed, "I would rather be a minister, but if this is where You want me, I will go." At that moment the peace of God swept over me and I knew God was speaking. All the lights were in focus. My initial guidance was sure.

When my wife, Judith and I arrived at the school we found the pamphlet had greatly misrepresented the facts. Besides having to pay the school for the privilege of working, the students worked eight, sometimes twelve, hours a day. This was above and beyond the six-hour classroom demand. We wanted to leave right away, but the Lord said, "Didn't I bring you here?"

I said, "Yes, Lord."

Delivered from Circumstances

Circumstances were seeking to dictate to us. Every day we mentally packed our bags to leave. Several times we literally packed only to unpack later. We knew our initial leading was correct according to the harbor lights. It was the only thing that kept us from panic and making a costly mistake.

The conflict within and without became almost unbearable. Finally we said, "God, You brought us here and the only way we will leave is for them to carry us out feet first." That ended the conflicts. Vacillation was replaced by genuine spiritual victory and peace in the midst of unfavorable circumstances. We both graduated with honors. The overall experience proved to be spiritual, rather than medical. Out of this, I came to know the ministry definition of *soul doctor*, realizing man's greatest conflicts are spiritual rather than physical.

As previously discussed, this same principle held true in the lives of the disciples. In the story of Jesus on the stormy sea as related in Mark 4:35-38, Jesus had spoken to the disciples saying, "Let us go over to the other side." However, Jesus fell asleep, and soon a mighty storm broke over the boat. The disciples were afraid. The waves were breaking into the boat, and it was filling with water.

These events compounded a frightening circumstance, and if the disciples had not remembered their initial leading, they would most likely have come to the conclusion that they were out of the will of God in a storm-tossed boat. But Jesus *had said*, "Let us pass over to the other side." *That* was the leading. No waves should cause them to turn back - and none did.

The enemy attacks many people by causing them to lose sight of their initial leading and become vulnerable to circumstances and impulses. Once we know where God is guiding, no matter what happens - hard times, suffering, poverty - we can *know* we are where God wants us.

If you ever lose sight of that initial leading, confusion will follow. If you begin to ask, "Should I have come here in the first place?" you might as well leave. If you do not know that God brought you, there is no foundation for any further leading.

Perhaps you have been asked to teach Sunday school. You pray, "Lord, do *You* want me to teach?"

"Yes, I want you to teach," comes the answer. Now if God wants you to teach, and you know that, then you can embrace the strain and difficulties from the superintendent, as well as the pressure from the children. Buckle down, stay with it, hold to your initial leading.

When the storm comes, Jesus will get the boat through. Are you in stormy waters with your husband or wife? Your boss? Your finances? Know your leading and place confidence in God's ability to complete that which He began (Phil 1:6).

Learning to Interpret

The Israelites were led out of Egypt, and the Lord promised to guide them to Canaan. But they lost their initial leading. They doubted that God was with them, and doubted that He would give them the promised land. They lost their way and wandered through the wilderness, tossed about by circumstances.

We must learn that *unfavorable* circumstances do not necessarily mean that we are *out* of God's will. Likewise we must learn that favorable circumstances are not necessarily a sign of being *in the will* of God.

The word of God came to Jonah, for instance, and commanded him to go to Nineveh and speak out against the wickedness of the city. But Jonah rebelled. He heard the word, he knew what God wanted, and he deliberately ran the other way. He intended to go to Tarshish to flee from the presence of the Lord. So he went down to Joppa and found the ship which "happened" to be ready to sail for Tarshish. He looked into his pocket and just "happened" to have the correct fare. Rejoicing in God's "provision of circumstance" alone, Jonah "knew" this was the will of God after all.

Imagine yourself in your study and suddenly the presence of the Lord says, "Arise, go to Los Angeles and speak out against the wickedness of that city!"

"Not me," you say, "I'm getting out of here. I will go to New York and get lost among the teeming millions. The Lord will never find me." So you run to the train station and there just happens to be a train leaving for New York in ten minutes. The fare is $184.50 and you just *happen* to have the right amount. "Glory to God, this must be the Lord helping me to run away," you reason.

Yet something happened to the ship Jonah sailed on. And something will sooner or later happen to you on the way to New York, even though at first the circumstances were *favorable* enough to be misleading.

A series of favorable circumstances may cause you to imagine that God is leading you when He is not. If someone falls in love with another man's wife and a series of favorable circumstances work out so that they are frequently left alone together. . . . Now wait a minute! Is that God's will?

Remember, *circumstances alone do not provide reliable guidance. They must line up with the other two harbor lights.* What does the Word of God say about falling in love with another man's wife? What about the Spirit of God? Can you commit adultery and still experience the peace of God?

We must not ignore or overlook circumstances. They are always a factor in guidance. But we need to see them in the right perspective. They *never* override Scripture and the peace of God.

CHAPTER
12
DESPISE NOT PROPHESYINGS!

Use and Abuse

Prophecy is one of the gifts of the Holy Spirit given to the Church for exhortation, edification, comfort, *and* guidance. In this study we are mainly concerned with the use of prophecy in personal guidance.

The prophets in the Old Testament foretold wars and famines, prosperity, and victories. Isaiah foretold the birth, life, death, and resurrection of Jesus with amazing accuracy. We readily accept the fact that God spoke through the prophets of old, but find it harder to believe that He can speak to us today in a similar way.

Prophecy is one of the charismas of the Church. A charisma is loosely defined as a special endowment of the Holy Spirit coming upon an individual to enable him to *know, do,* or *speak* in God's behalf as inspired by the Spirit. *The Holy Spirit is a restoration of the prophetic voice to the Church.*

In the book of Acts and letters to the young churches, we find that prophets served along with apostles and teachers. "And God has appointed in the church, first apostles, second prophets, third teachers, then miracles, then gifts of healings, helps, administrations, various kinds of tongues" (I Cor. 12:28).

Ground Rules

We know also that false prophets and the misuse of prophecy were rampant throughout the Bible and history of the Church. Because of their misuse of it, Paul found it necessary to carefully instruct the Corinthians in the use of prophecy. Apparently this gift, along with the gift of speaking in unknown tongues, had caused quite a controversy. Since a prophetic message often comes in an unknown tongue followed by interpretation, Paul discusses these two gifts together in his first letter to them. "And let two or three prophets speak, and let the others pass judgment. But if a revelation is made to another who is seated, let the first keep silent. For you can all prophesy one by one, so that all may learn and all may be exhorted; and the spirits of prophets are subject to prophets; for God is not a God of confusion but of peace, as in all the churches of the saints" (I Cor. 14:29-33).

Several important aspects of the use of prophecy are pointed out here. First, *the apostle lays down a ground rule for all guidance by prophecy:* "Let the others judge!" Paul's rule of safety is *never* to receive a prophecy which contains guidance while alone. Others should always be present to judge because the dangers of guidance received in this manner are very real. The advantages, however, surely outweigh the dangers. To the one who sincerely asks for the Holy Spirit, Jesus promised he would not be given a serpent! (Luke 11:11-15).

In Acts 11:27-30 we read: "During this period some prophets came down from Jerusalem to Antioch. One of them by the name of Agabus stood up and foretold by the

Spirit that there was to be a great famine throughout the world. (This actually happened in the days of Claudius.) The disciples determined to send relief to the brothers in Judaea, each contributing as he was able. This they did, sending their contribution to the elders there personally through Barnabas and Saul" (Phillips). Several prophets came to Antioch. When one spoke, others were there to judge. The message was an important one, and the disciples could not afford to make a mistake. Paul says to let the prophets speak.

Spirit of Prophecy

There is a difference between the office of the prophet and the spirit, or gift of prophecy. Paul says that obviously all are not called to be prophets, but there is such a thing as a spirit of prophecy that may rest on the entire congregation. On such an occasion, you and I may prophesy at times, this does not suggest we have a prophetic calling (I Cor. 12:28). Paul goes on to give advice to would-be prophets: "And the spirits of prophets are subject to prophets" (I Cor. 14:32).

Learning to Participate

We discussed earlier the three sources of wisdom: The supernatural wisdom from above which is peaceable and pure; the supernatural wisdom from below which is urgent, compulsive, bringing discord and strife; and, the third source of wisdom which is the human mind and emotions.

How do you and I learn to recognize when God wants us to open our mouth and speak a prophetic word? Over the years I have learned that the beginner usually experiences a physical exhilaration and quickening of the Holy Spirit in his body. Most often this is experienced as a heart-pounding or sense of excited expectation. Often I have said in a group meeting, "Will the person whose heart is pounding please obey the Lord." This is enough reassurance for him to recognize that the pounding heart or the fluttering stomach is often a prompting from God.

Knowing the Difference

However, an uncontrolled, compulsive message does not originate in God. The one who ministers and feels himself *carried away*, out of personal control, should begin to question the source and validity of what he is experiencing. The difference between the promptings of the Holy Spirit and the compulsion of other spirits (human or demonic) can be easily recognized. The Lord leads, draws, and prompts. Satan, or the human spirit, is always demanding, compelling, and pushing.

As you mature in the use of the gifts and ministries of the Holy Spirit, you can expect the exhilaration and physical sensation of the promptings of the Holy Spirit to diminish. You will learn how to respond in obedience to the gentle tugging of the Holy Spirit.

As stated, the misuse and abuse of prophecy has led many churches to abstain from the use of it. But today we are seeing a renewal of the use of the gifts of the Holy Spirit in all denominations of the Christian Church around the world. With this new emphasis comes a need to learn how to use these gifts properly.

Two Functions

Prophecy has two functions in personal guidance. One is directive, that is, it contains specific instructions about a course of action. This is the most common use of prophecy in guidance. The second is impartive, that is, by the laying on of hands and prophesying, the Holy Spirit imparts certain gifts or a specific calling to the believer. An example of this is found in I Timothy 4:14, "Do not neglect the spiritual gift within you, which was bestowed upon you through prophetic utterance with the laying on of hands by the presbytery."

Christians are too often forced to discover their calling or place in the Body of Christ by trial and error, rather than by means designated in the New Testament. This brings unnecessary trials and not a few errors.

Nine Scriptural Ways to Judge Prophecy

Prophecy is a supernatural form of guidance that can lead us into deception unless we learn to test the prophet and the prophecy. I have found nine distinct scriptural criteria for judging prophecy.

The Bible speaks of true and false prophets and gives us a criterion for testing them.

The first, and most obvious criterion for the truth or falsehood of a prophecy is its fulfillment. In Deuteronomy 18:20-22 we read: "But the prophet who shall speak a word presumptuously in My name which I have not commanded him to speak, or which he shall speak in the name of other gods, that prophet shall die. And you may say in your heart, '*How shall we know* the word which the Lord has spoken?'

When a prophet speaks in the name of the Lord, if the thing does not come about or come true, that is the thing which the Lord has not spoken. The prophet has spoken it presumptuously; you shall not be afraid of him."

A second factor is accompanying conditions. Most true prophecy in the realm of direction or foretelling is conditional. For example: "If you will take your place as a father and priest in your home, the Lord will bless you and preserve your children." If we do not meet the conditions, we cannot blame the prophet or God when the blessing does not come to pass.

Obviously there are times when we cannot wait for the fulfillment to prove a prophecy right or wrong. We need to know immediately if a prophetic message comes that says, "Thus saith the Lord, your city shall be destroyed," or "There shall be famine in the land." It is obvious that the disciples at Antioch did not wait for the famine to prove the prophecy. They acted upon it and sent supplies.

A third test or criterion is whether or not a prophecy is scriptural. If it is not in agreement with Scripture, it is false. No guidance is valid unless it conforms in essence to the written Word of God.

A prophetic message saying, "Divorce your wife and marry another," is obviously coming from a wrong source.

A fourth test concerns the public acknowledgment of the word. A prophecy spoken to you in privacy or in secret implying that you should *not tell it to others,* is often false. Remember, Paul said, *let others judge.*

I have seen some sad results of this form of misused or false prophecy. Beware of anyone who has a "word from the

Lord" to speak to you in private. A legitimate word of directive prophecy can come to you through a friend, but ask your friend to speak it openly where others can judge.

A fifth test of prophecy is that it should confirm something about which God has already spoken to you. The prophecy should come as confirmation. Other circumstances should fall into place and the prophecy should be the third harbor light of guidance lining up: the Holy Spirit speaking confirmation through prophecy.

The sixth test of prophecy is a witness to your inner spirit.

There is a much misquoted verse of Scripture, used most often by those who do not want to listen to the appointed teachers in the Church: "And as for you, the anointing which you received from Him abides in you, and you have no need for anyone to teach you; but as His anointing teaches you about all things, and is true and is not a lie, and just as it has taught you, you abide in Him" (I John 2:27).

John is talking about the Holy Spirit who abides in us and is our witness. How does He most often teach and guide us? By giving us an abiding peace about a matter, or a definite unrest. If the peace of God in our heart is upset by a prophetic message, we should exercise caution.

A seventh testing point concerns the purity of the vessel. The life of the prophet should agree with the prophecy. There are exceptions to this, and I have seen God use people who were living in open sin, people who were financially crooked or deceitful in other matters. But then, God also spoke truth through a donkey. Prophecy is a skill to be learned. Beginners always speak a mixture - part originating in God and the rest coming from the prophet's own human spirit.

As we conform to Christ, the purity of our message increases.

Learning to judge prophecy is also learning to judge the degree of mixture in a prophetic message, and to filter out the part that is not from the human spirit. A look at the degree of purity in the life of a prophet often gives us an indication of the purity of his message.

An eighth touchstone in judging prophecy is the spirit of the message itself. John said, "For the testimony of Jesus is the spirit of prophecy" (Rev. 19:10).

All true prophecy should be in the spirit and character of Jesus, the sender. It is never harsh, critical, or condemning. It may often be a message of rebuke, judgment, or conviction, but it is always just and given in mercy. An excellent example is found in Matthew 23:37 where Jesus mourns over Jerusalem: "Oh, Jerusalem, Jerusalem! You murder the prophets and stone the messengers that are sent to you. How often have I longed to gather your children round me like a bird gathering her brood together under her wings - and you would never have it" (Phillips).

A ninth criterion for true prophecy is a discerning of the burden of the Lord in the message. This is difficult to define, but it should be present in all true prophecy. In Jeremiah we read of the prophets who tried to please the people by crying, "Peace! Peace! when there was no peace."

There are prophetic messages in which one hears and senses the longing of God and His heavy burden for a straying or rebellious people. When this form of a message comes in a group meeting, the very spirit of it often makes the entire congregation break down and repent before the

Lord. Such prophecy is never a message of condemnation, but rather of intense yearning, as when God spoke to Solomon in II Chronicles 7:14, "And My people who are called by My name humble themselves and pray, and seek My face and turn from their wicked ways, then I will hear from heaven, will forgive their sin, and will heal their land." Simply stated, listen for *tears* in the voice and in the message.

All nine criteria *may* be present in a true prophetic message although this is not always so. Never accept a message as truth, however, unless some combination of these several criteria is present.

Remember, prophecy can be received and enjoyed. Fear and danger of deception can be avoided if we keep in mind these nine criteria:

1. Fulfillment
2. Accompanying conditions met
3. Scriptural agreement
4. Judgment of others
5. Confirmation
6. Spiritual witness
7. Purity of the vessel
8. Spirit of the message
9. Burden of the Lord

Evaluating prophecy and testing guidance should become second nature to us. Someone has said, "Open minds are like open windows; they need screens to keep the bugs out." We should not open our minds to prophecy until we know the message originates in God by the immediate application of the given criteria. We are responsible for what we receive. We should learn to discern the source.

Giving Prophecy Its Proper Place

A final word: Do not accept a prophecy on the basis of only one or two criteria. And then, even if you feel assured that the prophecy is true, do not accept guidance based on prophecy alone. Accept a prophecy only as *one* of the three harbor lights of guidance.

Misuse and abuse of the gift of prophecy have frightened many away from using it altogether. Paul urged the Corinthians, "Covet to prophesy," and told the Christians in Thessalonica, "Despise not prophesyings." But there must be a balance in prophecy. Some people give it *no place*, others give it *the place*, while God wants to give it *a place* in the life of the believer. In its proper place, prophecy is a tremendous tool in guidance.

CHAPTER
13
PROPHECY, ANGELS, VISIONS, AND DREAMS

Angels, visions, and dreams are not the common, every-day form of guidance. Throughout the pages of the Bible we find these forms of guidance used only in moments of crisis or crucial importance, when it was necessary for God to make an impact and establish a strong point of reference or an unshakable initial leading.

Angels

An angel named Gabriel appeared to Mary and told her she was to become the mother of Jesus.

A host of angels appeared to the shepherds in the field and announced the good news of the Savior's birth. They instructed the shepherds to go to Bethlehem and told them where to find the child.

An angel was sent to Cornelius to give guidance about sending for Peter who would bring the message of life (Acts 10:1-8).

The Lord spoke to Ananias in a vision and told him to go to the house of Judas on the street called Straight and inquire there for a man named Saul of Tarsus, "for behold, he is praying, and he has seen in a vision a man named Ananias come in and lay his hands on him, so that he might regain his sight" (Acts 9:11-13). Ananias did not like the assignment and reminded the Lord of Saul's record, "How much harm he did to Thy saints at Jerusalem" (vs. 13). But the Lord assured Ananias that Saul was a chosen vessel who would bear the name of the Lord before Gentiles, kings, and the children of Israel. God spoke in a vision both to Ananias and to Saul because they needed a strong point of reference.

I have heard people say, "Oh, if God would only speak to me the way He spoke to Saul when He struck him down, blinded him with a terrible light, and spoke to him in a loud voice."

Why did God speak in such a spectacular way to Saul? Possibly there were two reasons. First, because Saul probably had been running from God's voice for some time. He had been a witness to the stoning of Stephen and was so stirred up by the Gospel that he became an ardent persecutor of all who confessed the name of Jesus Christ. Saul was not lukewarm; he was in hot pursuit of the Christians. Yet at the same time the spirit of conviction was burning in his heart. God had to speak to Saul in a spectacular way because he was blind and deaf to the still, small voice of God. *The principle in unusual guidance is that the farther we are from God, the louder He may have to speak.*

A Strong Point of Reference

The second reason was the need for a strong point of reference in Saul's life, something he would never forget! God told Ananias in the vision, "For I will show him (Saul) how he must suffer for My name's sake" (vs. 16). Paul was beaten, jailed, stoned, and left for dead for the sake of the

Gospel. But God had spoken to him *in proportion to the degree of challenge he would face.* Paul had dreams, visions, saw angels, heard voices, and was caught up into the third heaven. And he never forgot what happened to him on the road to Damascus.

An End in Itself

What happens when someone accepts prophetic utterance, has a vision, sees an angel, or has a dream? Often, the experience becomes an end in itself. It can become a trap for the Christian who may spend the next several years talking about it, rather than using the experience as a means to an end.

A minister whom I had known, experienced a vision. God spoke to him very distinctly. For twenty-five years the minister preached the same vision. He never moved beyond it.

Prophecy, angels, visions, and dreams are scriptural forms of guidance, but if we make them an end instead of the means to the end, we have missed the point completely. Having dreams, visions, and seeing angels are not necessarily a mark of spirituality. Paul stated the ultimate goal for us as Christians to be, "That I may know Him . . ." (Phil. 3:10). Our goal is to *know* Jesus Christ and to share His suffering and His resurrection, not necessarily to have three-hour visions, spectacular dreams, or angelic visitors in our bedroom!

Insofar as angels, dreams, and visions are made subservient to the known scriptural goal, they are useful. These spectacular forms of guidance function as the scaffolding on a new building. But to become absorbed in the experience (scaffolding) and fail to build the building is a deception of the worst kind.

Angels *are* real. They appear throughout the Bible as messengers, guardians, and comforters. They minister to the saints, warn against danger, fight in battles, and will return in triumph with Jesus when He returns in glory!

An angel opened the prison doors for the apostles in Jerusalem and told them to go to the Temple and preach the Word of God. Another angel awoke Peter when he was in prison and told him to arise and go. But are we to believe an angel if he comes to us?

Paul warned the Galatians, "But even though we, or an angel from heaven, should preach to you a gospel contrary to that which we have preached to you, let him be accursed" (Gal. 1:8).

Peter says angels are subject to Biblical revelation and if an angel speaks contrary to the written Word of God, he is a false angel. Thus an angelic messenger must be treated like any other avenue of guidance. We test the message as we would test a prophecy or any other leading. The written Word of God is the first criterion, but even if the angel should give a message that we find in agreement with the Scriptures, the rule of the three harbor lights still stands. The peace of God and the circumstances must line up.

An angel may be a beautiful apparition and should he come into our room, might even overwhelm us with his powerful light and wisdom. But Paul reminds us that "Satan disguises himself as an angel of light" (II Cor. 11:14).

We are told in Acts 2:17 that prophecy, dreams, and visions are to be part of our Christian experience. "'And it shall be in the last days,' God says, 'That I will pour forth of My Spirit upon all mankind; and your sons and your daughters shall prophesy, and your young men shall see visions, and your old men shall dream dreams.'" This is a quote from the prophet Joel, which, when quoted by Peter, takes on new meaning for the serious Christian.

A vision is a direct illumination from God and is often used as guidance in the Bible.

Spectacular Forms of Guidance

Twice in a row, Paul was hindered by the Holy Spirit when he tried to preach the word of God in Asia. Finally God sent a vision to Paul in the night, "A certain man of Macedonia was standing and appealing to him, and saying, 'Come over to Macedonia and help us.' And when he had seen the vision, immediately we sought to go into Macedonia, concluding that God had called us to preach the gospel to them" (Acts 16:9-10).

Why such a spectacular form of guidance? Possibly God had spoken to Paul by the Holy Spirit earlier, but Paul had not quite understood. But also, Paul and Silas were probably going to need a strong point of reference. The principle is that God must speak to us in direct proportion to the challenge we will face in the future. In Macedonia they went to Philippi and there they were badly beaten and thrown into jail. Had they gone to Philippi without being certain of their guidance, the circumstances of being beaten and thrown into jail might have caused them to doubt their initial guidance.

Instead, deep in the inner prison with their feet fastened against the dungeon walls, Paul and Silas prayed and sang praises to God until midnight. Suddenly an earthquake shook the foundations of the prison, all the doors were opened, and everyone's irons were loosed. Certain he had lost his prisoners, the jailer was about to throw himself against his sword when Paul shouted, "Do not harm yourself; we are all here."

The jailer was so amazed that he cried out to Paul and Silas, "What must I do to be saved?" They told him and he received Jesus Christ as his Savior. He then took the prisoners home, washed their wounds, and he and his entire family submitted themselves to water baptism that night as an outward sign of their belief.

What an amazing story! It teaches us the principle that when God sends a vision as exceptional guidance we may expect some adverse circumstances ahead.

Preparation for Ministry

A vision may be given to *prepare* us for a certain ministry. In Acts 10 we read about Peter who went up on the housetop to pray. There he had a vision. He saw something like a great sheet being lowered from heaven. In it were all kinds of beasts, creeping things, and birds - things Jews were not allowed to eat. A voice told Peter to rise, kill, and eat. But Peter refused, saying, "By no means, Lord, for I have never eaten anything unholy and unclean." A third time the voice spoke to him saying, "What God has cleansed, no longer consider unholy." Then the vision disappeared.

While Peter was wondering what all that meant, some men knocked on the door downstairs and asked for him. They had been sent by Cornelius, a Roman centurion in the city of Caesarea. Cornelius had fasted and prayed until an angel from God told him to send for Peter. When Peter heard what the men had to say, he suddenly realized what the vision had been about. He went with the men to Cornelius's house where many Gentiles were gathered to hear the Word of God.

Peter told them, "You all know that it is forbidden for a man who is a Jew to associate with, or even visit, a man of another nation. But God has shown me plainly that no man must be called 'common' or 'unclean.' That is why I came here . . . without objection" (Acts 10:28-29 Phillips).

God had prepared Peter for his ministry to the Gentiles by giving him a strong point of reference. Later he was asked to explain his action to some of the disciples in Jerusalem who were full of criticism. When Peter told them of his vision and how it was confirmed in his experience with Cornelius, they had no further objection.

One day a dairyman in Southern California was in his room praying. Suddenly, he saw a vision. Multitudes of businessmen were being swept into the Kingdom of God. While the vision was taking place, his wife came in and stood beside him. She began explaining to him simultaneously everything he saw, just as he saw it. It was a double witness. This man founded a fellowship of Holy Spirit filled businessmen, which has grown to international stature.

The vision became his strong point of reference in times of doubt and testing.

A vision can come as a warning of danger. During World War II a lady in England was sitting in church one Sunday morning. Suddenly she had a vision of the church being destroyed in an explosion. She jumped to her feet and told the congregation. The pastor decided to clear the church immediately. A short while later, a V-2 rocket fell and destroyed the building.

Can spectacular guidance come from a source other than God? Of course, and it must be put to the same test as other forms of guidance. Is it scriptural? Does it reveal or impart knowledge and wisdom that is pure, peaceable, and approachable? Or would it cause disharmony and rivalry? If so, it is not of God. In the name of Jesus Christ it should be refused.

A friend of mine was teaching in a home prayer meeting when suddenly he saw a clear vision of a large tin can standing on a shelf in a barn. Someone was putting pieces of silver into the can. My friend could see the picture in detail, down to a crooked nail on the shelf next to the can. The vision recurred three times, and at last my friend stopped teaching, looked at the group of people sitting around the room and said, "I don't know what this means, but I am seeing someone putting away silver in a can. The Lord is telling me that the person is hoarding his money."

Across the room a man began to cry. "Oh, my," he explained, "I have been sitting here wondering if I was supposed to give that money to the Lord. I prayed and told the Lord that if you said anything about the money, I would obey."

He insisted that my friend go with him after the meeting. They went out to his barn, where for years he had been secretly hiding his money (all in quarters and half-dollars) in a can on the shelf. My friend looked, and beside the can was the crooked nail.

The vision was a strong point of reference for the man who had been holding money back from his family for years. You may cheat your wife, your boss, or the government, but God sees your hidden treasure.

Dreams

Dreams are not mentioned very often in the New Testament. However, they are frequently mentioned in the Old Testament. An angel appeared to Joseph in a dream, telling him that Mary was to become the mother of God's own Son. When the wise men had brought their gifts to the baby in the manger, they were warned in a dream not to report the whereabouts of the child to Herod. Again in a dream, Joseph was told to flee to Egypt, and in another dream he was told that Herod was dead and he could safely return with Mary and the child to Nazareth.

Dreams have a place in guidance, but take care; dreams can come from eating chocolate-covered dill pickles! My brother-in-law was able to control his dreams in a nightly series by what he ate prior to going to bed. Indigestion, tension, fear, and other pressures can cause some weird dreams. Put your dream to the test. If it is from God, it should pass the criteria for true guidance.

I have had a few dreams in my life which I knew originated in God. I have had hundreds which did not! If a dream is of God, it is often meant to be a point of reference, a preparation for a time of testing.

Once I dreamed that I was walking through heavy brush and briars. They were pulling and tearing my clothes and skin. Finally I was through the thicket and discovered that before me was an insurmountable rock wall. I stood there in dazed helplessness and cried, "Oh Jesus! Help me!" Suddenly, off to my right, I discovered a small crevice just big enough for me to squeeze through. I struggled through the rock, and on the other side was a beautiful blue expanse of clear water. I slipped down into the softness, and suddenly it was as if I was in the arms of Jesus. I woke up in the morning praising God. I said, "Thank you, Jesus, for showing me that everything is going to be all right." This dream I knew was from the Lord.

For the next few months we went through some heavy briars and brush of trials and circumstances and finally, there it was, the insurmountable wall! I said, "Thank You for the mountain, Lord; now where is that crevice?" I knew in my heart it was there, and I just waited calmly for the Lord. Suddenly, there it was and I slipped through the crevice.

Dream Books

What if instead I had purchased a dream-book and looked up the symbolic meaning of "water" and "rocks"? Beware of such books as well as some of the dream-interpreters, for they border on the realm of fortune-telling and the world of the psychic.

God sent my dream to prepare me and protect me. I could have missed the point and opened myself wide to destructive wisdom from the Satanic realm. The result would have been confusion, and I could have "missed the mark" for my life and ministry.

Prophecy, angels, visions, and dreams have their place in guidance, but only as they fall into line with the other criteria of guidance. We must take another look, for unusual guidance is only a means to an end; that we may know Christ and find our place in His Kingdom.

CHAPTER
14
SIGNS AND FLEECES

Accommodation and Unbelief

God often gives a visible sign as a symbol or token of something He wants us to understand. When Moses was shepherding his father-in-law's flock near Mount Horeb, God called to him out of the burning bush, "Go and gather the elders of Israel together, and say to them, the Lord, the God of your fathers, the God of Abraham, Isaac, and Jacob, has appeared to me saying, 'I am indeed concerned about you and what has been done to you in Egypt.' So I said, 'I will bring you up out of the affliction of Egypt to the land . . . flowing with milk and honey'" (Ex. 3:16-17).

Moses said, "But Lord, they will not believe me!"

To accommodate the unbelief of the Israelites, God gave Moses three *signs* to show them. *First,* the sign of the rod. Thrown on the ground, the rod would become a serpent. The serpent would become a rod again when Moses picked it up by the tail.

Second, the sign of the hand. Moses would put his hand into his bosom and withdraw it. It would be leprous and white as snow. Again, Moses would put his hand into his bosom and withdraw it. Now, it would be restored and whole.

Third, the sign of the water turning to blood. God told Moses, "If they will not believe you, or heed the voice or the testimony of the first sign, they may believe the voice or the witness of the second sign. But, if they will also not believe these two signs or heed your voice, you shall take some water of the river [Nile], and pour it upon the dry land; and the water . . . shall become blood" (Ex. 4:1-9 Amplified).

Moses and Aaron went to Egypt and performed the signs God had given them. These were supernatural demonstrations that could not be performed by the natural power or ability of man. And the signs were given to generate faith.

Three Categories of Signs

We find three categories of signs in the Bible.

One, the *supernatural* working of wonders and miracles which are a demonstration of God's power in response to man's unbelief.

Two, the *allegorical* sign that foretells the nature of a coming event or judgment.

Three, a *natural* sign, such as the appearance of a star to signify that a promise or a prediction is about to be fulfilled.

The Lord commanded Isaiah to take off his robe and sandals and walk naked and barefoot for three years as a sign to the Egyptians and Ethiopians. This was a sign to show how they would be led away captive, naked, and barefoot by the Assyrians (Isa. 20:2-4).

We may be encouraged to watch for signs. Isaiah says, "Therefore the Lord Himself will give you a *sign*: Behold, a virgin will be with child, and bear a son, and she will call His name Immanuel" (Isa. 7:14). The shepherds in the field near Bethlehem were told of the birth of the child, and the angels said, "And this will be a sign for you: you will find a baby wrapped in cloth, and lying in a manger" (Luke 2:12).

Jesus tells us that certain signs shall follow those who believe on Him, "In My name they will cast out demons, they will speak with new tongues; they will pick up serpents, and if they drink any deadly poison, it shall not hurt them; they will lay hands on the sick, and they will recover" (Mark 16:17-18). In the book of Acts, we see those signs did indeed follow the believers. And since Jesus is the same today as He was yesterday, and since His commands are timeless, we can discover these same signs still following the believers today.

The Use of Signs in Guidance

Is it then scriptural to ask for a sign when we want to be certain that God is speaking to us? Here again, caution needs to be exercised. A sign *can* be a scriptural form of guidance, but it is rarely sufficient when given alone. The same rules for confirmation apply to signs as to the other forms of guidance. The sign should conform with the written Word of God, witness with the peace of God in our heart, and with the circumstances (the three harbor lights).

Jesus was often asked for signs. In Matthew 12:38-40 we read, "Then some of the scribes and Pharisees answered Him, saying, 'Teacher, we want to see a sign from you.' But He answered and said to them, 'An evil and adulterous generation craves for a sign; and yet *no sign* will be given to it but the sign of Jonah the prophet; for as Jonah was three days and three nights in the belly of the sea monster, so shall the Son of Man be three days and three nights in the heart of the earth.'" Thus when Jesus spent three days in the grave, the Pharisees and the scribes did not believe, although the sign had been given them.

Inward Dispositions

Again and again we read in the Bible that many signs were given, but the people did not understand them. They were blind and deaf to the messages God sought to convey.

There is often in us an inward disposition that blinds us to the truth, even when we see a clear sign. I once witnessed a remarkable healing. A woman had a large goiter on her neck, and a man laid hands on her and prayed that God would remove it. Almost instantly the goiter disappeared, leaving the skin hanging loose. My first reaction was one of unbelief, "That man must be a phony," I said to myself. There was in me an *unwillingness* to believe, regardless of the · evidence.

As long as there is an inward disposition to not believe, it makes no difference what God does or does not do in the way of signs. Jesus Christ performed wonders, signs, and miracles every day; yet many who saw with their own eyes and heard with their own ears refused to believe.

When God gives us a sign, it is because He wants us to see something or do something. The first condition is that we be *willing* to be shown, even if it is something new and demanding. Even then, Jesus' word to the Scribes and Pharisees (and to Thomas who wanted to see the nail marks in His hands) was that it is much better when we believe without a sign. Why is that? Because a sign can be imitated. As mature Christians we should walk in faith, *not following signs.* The New Testament says the signs should follow us - not that we should follow the signs (Mark 16:20).

Counterfeit Signs

Moses and Aaron performed signs to show the power of God. Pharaoh called in his magicians who were able to perform *the very same signs.* They threw down the rods that turned into serpents, they copied the sign of leprosy and of water turning into blood. Initially, Satan was able to counterfeit each one of God's signs - which is one of the primary reasons all signs must be checked against the other harbor lights.

There is a warning in Deuteronomy against false prophets who may give a sign or a wonder, "And [if] the sign or the wonder comes true, concerning which he spoke to you, saying, 'Let us go after other gods (whom you have not known) and let us serve them,' you shall not listen to the words of that prophet . . ." (Deut. 13:2-3).

False prophets, then, also produce signs that will come to pass. Jesus tells us in Matthew 24:24, "For there shall arise false Christs, and false prophets, and shall show great signs and wonders, so as to mislead, if possible, even the elect."

The power behind these false signs is Satan himself: "The one whose coming is in accord with the activity of Satan, with all power and signs and false wonders" (II Thess. 2:9). Does that include the same kind of signs Jesus talked about in Mark 16; such as healings, casting out of demons, and speaking in tongues? Yes, it does. These things can be and are being counterfeited by Satan. This is why biblical guidance is so necessary.

God's purpose is to bring us beyond the point where we need signs to discern His guiding hand. Satan cannot counterfeit the peace of God or the love of God dwelling in us. When Christ's abiding presence becomes our guide, then guidance becomes an almost unconscious response to the gentle moving of His Holy Spirit within us. But this is the ideal form of guidance, and there is often a great difference between the real and the ideal.

Final Answers

Signs are given to us, because God meets us on the level where we operate. Signs are also given through us to generate faith among unbelievers. As such, the signs and wonders are a fulfillment of God's promise in the Scriptures. In guidance, when God shows us a sign, it does not mean we have received the final answer. A sign means we are on the way. On the highway we may pass a sign saying, "Tulsa 100 miles." The sign does not mean we have reached Tulsa, but it tells us we are on the right road.

Gideon and His Fleece

There is an amazing story of God's patience and willingness to accommodate our need for signs and fleeces in Judges 6.

The scene opens with Gideon threshing wheat behind a winepress. Those were hard days for the Israelites. They had done evil in the sight of the Lord, and He had delivered them into the hands of their enemies the Midianites who had occupied their land for seven years and taken all their harvest. Gideon was doing the threshing behind the winepress to hide from the Midianites. Suddenly, he was aware of the angel of the Lord sitting under an oak tree, watching him. The angel said, "The Lord is with you, O valiant warrior."

Gideon retorted, "If the Lord is with us, why then has all this happened to us? And where are all His miracles which our fathers told us about, saying, 'Did not the Lord bring us up from Egypt?' But now the Lord has abandoned us and given us into the hand of Midian" (Judg. 6:12-13). Gideon was a typical second-generation skeptic. He had heard the big tales of what God had done in the old days. But where was the evidence now? Gideon's people were all living in caves and dens, hiding from the powerful enemy.

The angel had a message for Gideon. He told him the Lord wanted to send him to save Israel from the hand of the Midianites. At this, Gideon replied, "Oh, Lord, how can I deliver Israel? Behold, my clan is the poorest in Manasseh, and I am the least in my father's house." The Lord said to him, "Surely I will be with you, and you shall smite the Midianites as one man" (Judg. 6:15-16 Amplified).

By now Gideon had begun to wonder what was going on. He said to the angel, "If now I have found favor in Your sight, then show me a sign that it is You Who talks with me" (Judg. 6:17 Amplified).

First God spoke by an angel, but Gideon was not satisfied. He wanted a sign and told the angel to wait while he went to prepare an offering. He returned with a sacrifice of meat and unleavened bread, and the angel told him to put the meat and bread on a rock and pour the broth from the meat over it. Then the angel reached out and touched the meat and the bread with the tip of his staff and fire flared up from the rock, consuming the meat and the bread. Thereafter, the angel vanished from Gideon's sight leaving him convinced. "Alas, O Lord God!" he said. "For now I have seen the Angel of the Lord face to face!" (Judg. 6:22 Amplified).

Yet the very next day we see that doubt has entered Gideon. He has had to face some adverse circumstances and opposition from his own people and now he turns to God for additional reassurance, "If You will deliver Israel by my hand *as You have said,* behold I will put a fleece of wool on the threshing floor; if there is dew on the fleece only, and it is dry on all the ground, then I shall know that You will deliver Israel by my hand, *as You have said*" (Judg. 6:36-37 Amplified).

Gideon already knew the will of God. He had seen the angel and the sign. He was convinced that God was the one who had said that He would deliver Israel by Gideon's hand. But he was not absolutely sure that God could do what He had promised to do. Gideon wanted more proof.

Divine Displeasure

The next morning Gideon got up and checked the fleece. When he squeezed it, there was a whole bowl full of water. Now, surely, Gideon was reassured. But no, he turned right around and asked for another sign, "Let not Your *anger* be kindled against me, and I will speak but this once; let me make trial only this once with the fleece, I pray; let it now be dry only upon the fleece, and upon all the ground let there be dew" (Judg. 6:39 Amplified).

Gideon knew that he incurred the risk of divine displeasure by insisting on testing God when he already knew the answer. Gideon said, "Please don't be angry God. I just want one more sign!"

In the next verse we see that God did not get angry. In patience He accommodated Gideon's weakness and insecurity, "And God did so that night, for it was dry on the fleece only, and there was dew on all the ground" (Judg. 6:40 Amplified).

Fleecing is a "popular" form of guidance with many, but if we read the story of Gideon there can be no doubt that *the fleece was not a divinely ordained means of guidance.* It was simply God's accommodation to the weakness of men. Not only that, but in all the Scripture we find this method used only once.

Most of our "fleeces" are excuses for laziness or cowardice. We say, "I'll just put out a fleece. Lord, if You want me to go to work tomorrow, let the newspaper be on my front porch instead of in the yard." Remember, God had already called Gideon. He knew Gideon's willingness. But most of us are unwilling and use the fleece method simply to rationalize away the requirements of obedience.

Fleeces or Circumstances

If you feel that you need to use a fleece for guidance, be sure you ask for one that requires supernatural intervention beyond the possibility of any natural circumstances. What we call fleeces are often not fleeces at all, but fall into the category of circumstances.

When Jonah ran from the presence of the Lord, we can imagine him saying, "Now Lord, if You want me to run away from You, just arrange to have a boat at Joppa ready to sail for Tarshish and I will take that as a sign." That is not a fleece, that is circumstance. We have learned that the written Word of God and the Holy Spirit giving us the peace of God must always line up with the circumstances (the three harbor lights).

Gideon knew the will of God beyond any doubt *before* he put out his fleeces. God accommodated him in his weakness because he was going to need an extraordinary point of reference. Gideon was required to meet the powerful army of the Midianites with only a handful of Israelites. God gave him sufficient signs, so he would not forget, even for a moment, what God was able to do.

The Exception and the Norm

Gideon's experience is the exception, not the norm in guidance. Let it be understood that I know that in our spiritual youthfulness and immaturity, God has honored and does honor many things which we put out as a "fleece." If we *know* what God is asking of us and still insist on laying out fleeces, we may open ourselves to deception. Maturity demands that we learn to be guided by the Holy Spirit.

If I have a wife and meet another woman and fall in love, I may say, "Dear Lord, if You want me to have two wives, show me." It is in instances like this that the confused bigamist later testifies that he had an angelic visitor who told him, "Thus saith the Lord, thou shall take two wives. You will be like Solomon, great in wisdom and with many wives!" I have chosen an extreme example to bring home an important point.

Florida or California Oranges

I know people who are in doubt about a course of action and they "fleece" the Lord, "Lord, I do not know whether You want me to move to Florida or California. The next time I go to the store I will buy a bag of oranges, and if You want me to go to Florida, let it be a bag of Florida oranges. If You want me to go to California, let it be a bag of California oranges."

Ridiculous! If you are in that kind of dilemma, you ought to use the sanctified intellect Paul used when he set out to preach in Asia. He tried, but the Holy Spirit prevented him. If you do not know where to go, but you know you are not supposed to stay where you are, tell the Lord, "I want to do Your will. Therefore, I am going to start out in this direction and if You do not want me to go there, close the door, Lord, and show me another one." This is *circumstantial guidance* and it is scriptural.

The need for signs and fleeces arises from our unbelief. *God will accommodate us while we are in the process of learning to discern His will.* But counterfeit signs and answers to fleecing may deceive us, and we must learn never to take guidance from these evidences alone.

CHAPTER
15
ONE STEP AT A TIME

Confidence or Dependence

We usually think that the more we learn to understand and practice the principles of guidance, the more confident and self-assured we will become. I have discovered, in practice, that *the very opposite is true.* The longer I walk with God, the less self-sufficient I become, and the more subjectively dependent I am upon God. Now if that is the case, who wants to be guided?

Jesus said, "I am the vine, you are the branches; he who abides in Me, and I in him, he bears much fruit; for apart from Me you can do nothing" (John 15:5). The more we permit God to work in our life, the more He will strip us of the tendency we have to attempt spiritual fruit-bearing on our own.

Most all of God's dealings in our life are designed to destroy our dependence upon ourselves. This is one of the reasons guidance must be a *step-by-step* proposition. If we could know all that is to happen, we would become cocky and forget our total dependence on God. Proverbs 4:11 says, "I have taught you in the way of skillful and godly Wisdom [which is comprehensive insight into the ways and purposes of God]; I have led you in paths of uprightness" (Amplified). God is not talking to beginners here. He says,

"I *have* taught you . . . ." Now look at verse 12, "When you walk, your steps shall not be hampered . . . ." This Hebrew word 'walk' is better translated, 'step-by-step.'

Candles or Halogen Lamp

In Columbia, South America, the people walk to church meetings on narrow paths through the jungle. They carry a crude lamp made from a tin can with a candle in it, and by flickering candlelight, they walk through the dark jungle, step by step.

We would not like going through the jungle with that type of lamp. We prefer the halogen lamp, which would enable us to see a puma or a boa constrictor far ahead of us. We would want to be prepared. When we talk that way, what we are actually saying is, "I am really capable of handling *any* situation as long as I am properly prepared!" This is self-deception in its arrogant form.

Psalm 119:105 says, "Thy word is a lamp to my feet, and a light to my path." Walk one step at a time, God is saying, with a flickering homemade lamp that does not light up the road three miles ahead like an halogen lamp.

Knowing the Future

When we walk with God, we learn that guidance is seldom given all at once. The Lord may say, "I want you to go into the insurance business."

"But Lord, what does the *future* hold?" you ask.

God says, "That is My business, don't worry about it."

Maybe we have had a dream or embraced circumstantial guidance in such a way that we feel we have *already* interpreted the future. This results in a false sense of assurance. Guidance, which has importance for the future, *almost always comes in seed form*. As a seed, it unfolds one aspect at a time, and you will recognize it as it does. The daily outworking, however, is still a step-by-step walk in faith. When we are unable to plan the outcome, some of our self-dependence is destroyed, and we learn to depend more on God.

Spiritual Maturity

King Solomon was known for his wisdom, but in I Kings 3:7 he says, "O Lord my God, . . . I am but a lad [in wisdom and experience]; I know not how to go out [begin] or come in [finish]" (Amplified).

This same Solomon said in Proverbs 20:24, "Man's steps are ordered by the Lord; how can a man then understand his way?" (Amplified).

The prophet Jeremiah cried out: "I know, O Lord, that a man's way is not in himself; nor is it in a man who walks to direct his steps. Correct me, O Lord, but with justice; not with Thine anger, lest Thou bring me to nothing" (Jer. 10:23-24). Jeremiah knew the heart of God.

When we have been taught the principles of walking with God, it is necessary that we submit to this stripping of *self-dependence* and *self-determination*. If we do not, there is the possibility, as Jeremiah said, that we may be brought to nothing.

The goal is a childlike dependence on God, and the characteristics of one possessing a childlike spirit are that he is both *hungry* and *teachable*. Thus a mark of spiritual maturity is a childlike spirit. If that sounds like a contradiction, it is because we have developed a wrong philosophy of spiritual maturity. We think of the spiritually mature leader as one who is bold and confident, speaking with the voice of authority, making everyone tremble in fear and respect. This is our mental picture of the Apostle Paul. Let us remember, it is this man who taught us the difference between child-like and childish! (I Cor. 13:11 with I Cor. 14:20).

Paul's picture of himself is a very different one. He writes to the Corinthians, "And I was with you in weakness and in fear and in much trembling. And my message and my preaching were not in persuasive words of wisdom, but in demonstration of the Spirit and of power" (I Cor. 2:3-4).

Is that how we want to be? That is where God wants us.

Growing in maturity means we must no longer base our relationship with God on *feelings*. FAITH is the key word in Christianity. By FAITH we are saved. By FAITH we are baptized in the Holy Spirit. By FAITH we are healed. By FAITH we are guided. We can never mature in our Christian experience as long as we are overly dependent on outward feelings and sensations. If *that* is our foundation, one day the whole building may come tumbling down.

Tunnel Experiences

It is essential that we allow God to strip us of our *dependency* on feelings. To accomplish that, God takes us through what may be called a tunnel experience. In the tunnel there is very little emotion. It is dark all around and we say, "Lord, are You still with me?" There is no answer.

But I do have my flickering candle-lamp: What does my Bible say?

"Thy Word is a lamp unto my feet, a light unto my path." So there it is, God's Word. I'm going to have to learn to trust God's Word, regardless of how I feel.

Jesus said, "I will never leave you nor forsake you." Even here in the long black tunnel where I do not feel His presence or hear His voice, He's here! The Lord has chosen to remove the *sense* of His presence, and not the presence itself.

What if I panic? I have been in tunnels where I panicked and found the Lord right next to me asking, "Did you call?"

"Yes, Lord. I just wanted to be sure You meant it when You said You wouldn't leave me."

"Of course, I am here. I will reconfirm My presence to you so you will *feel* better."

But what happens now? The tunnel must be extended, because what God wanted to accomplish in my life was interrupted by my *panic at the absence of feeling*. The tunnel experience is designed to strip us of the outward and soulish dependency on emotionalism, which is anything but faith.

There are some who are unwilling to go through the tunnel. They panic halfway through, "Lord, please, I do not feel spiritual anymore; I want to feel You, Lord. I want to back out of this faith-walk."

There is no condemnation for those who want to remain on this side of the tunnel. But neither is there maturity. Paul scolded some New Testament Christians, "You are old enough to eat meat, but you are still drinking milk. When you ought to be teaching others, you are still being taught."

Once you come through the tunnel, there is new light on the other side, a deeper understanding of God's Word, a stronger faith, and with it, increased responsibility for what we have learned.

The principle is the same in guidance. Unless we are willing to be stripped of our dependence on outward signs and manifestations, we will never be able to go on into maturity. *Walking in mature obedience reduces the necessity for the obvious and more spectacular forms of guidance.* That does not mean God no longer speaks to us in prophecy or through visions or angels or in an audible voice if He so chooses. *Being stripped of our dependency on feeling does not mean we will no longer be aware of God's presence.* It means we are no longer depending on it. Our mature faith is based on fact, not feeling.

Why are we not exposed to all truth at once? Why can't God just show us the map and say, "This is where you are going to walk and this is what is going to happen"? One reason God does not reveal all truth to us at one time is because it would cause us to withdraw from total dependency on Him. Another reason is that knowledge of the truth makes us responsible for it. Both of these require a certain maturity which needs to be cultivated. Jesus told His disciples that there were things they simply could not bear to hear at this time (John 16:12).

We are responsible for the truth we know. We are responsible for the guidance we receive. If we *know* the truth, *know* what God wants us to do, and deliberately ignore it or rebel, we discover a different *kind* of accountability. It should be clear that we need time. It is not possible to mature "overnight," even if we are totally yielded to God and believe that we are willing to do anything for Him.

The Time Factor

Maturity takes time. Do not confuse the terms "mature" and "immature" with "perfect" and "imperfect." A child can be a perfect child although he is not a mature adult. The immature rosebud is just as perfect as the full-blooming rose. The lamb is as perfect as the sheep. The only difference is the *time factor.*

Sheep and Lambs

The Scripture speaks a great deal about sheep, lambs, and shepherds. We know Jesus as "the Good Shepherd," and He refers to believers as sheep and lambs. In John 10:27 Jesus said, "My *sheep* hear My voice," not, "My *lambs* hear My voice."

There is an illustration about two shepherds who let their flocks graze and drink water together. When it came time to part, one of the shepherds called for his sheep to follow him, and right away the sheep in his flock came out from among the others. The sheep knew their shepherds' voice. But what about the lambs? The lambs followed the sheep, of course.

When we are first born in Jesus' flock, we are lambs, and we follow the sheep. Then, little by little, as we associate with the Shepherd, we begin to know His voice for ourselves. By the time we are sheep, we are ready to follow Him and lead others along. The responsibility of the sheep is a grave one. When a sheep (the more mature believer) strays from the flock, lambs are apt to follow and get lost.

In the Christian community, the young Christians who are unable to discern the Lord's voice as yet, say, "Oh, I will just listen to my pastor; he is mature in God." If that pastor is not following the voice of his Shepherd, his flock will end up in the ditch. In God's plan, this is as well, the role of the husband and father in a household. Families are shipwrecked and tragedies occur when the man in the house refuses to follow the guidance and direction of God so that he can lead his little flock.

Have you ever heard of the "Judas sheep" in the stockyards? When a new flock of sheep comes in to be slaughtered, the Judas sheep is let in among them in the pen. Because he is specially trained, he soon wins their confidence and leads them toward the slaughterhouse. Just as they get to the gate, he jumps aside and the other sheep continue on to the slaughter. The responsibility of leadership is an awesome one.

Pray that as a more mature Christian you may lead the other sheep and the lambs to the Shepherd. That, after all, is our objective - fellowship with the Shepherd. God desires that we mature into sheep who know His voice. There are some who would rather be lambs all their life, just being fed and led, avoiding responsibility! But maturity is learning to feed yourself, and in turn helping to feed others. Maturity is producing more than we consume.

Passing the Initiative

In our society we have been conditioned to think of maturity in terms of independence. Young people are told, "When you become mature, you can be independent."

Spiritual maturity is the very opposite. God does not tell us, "Now son, when you are grown and spiritually mature, you are on your own. You make your own decisions. You can choose your own vocation. You are old enough to have a life of your own and a home of your own."

Jesus said to Peter, "I assure you . . . when you were young, you girded yourself - put on your own belt (girdle) - and you walked about wherever you pleased to go. But when you grow old you will stretch out your hands and someone else will put a girdle around you, and carry you where you do not wish to go" (John 21:18 Amplified).

In my early life I was so full of zeal and eagerness that I went everywhere holding meetings. Jesus simply went with me. It was where I wanted to go. Then one memorable day when the Lord knew I was old enough, I rushed ahead to a certain city in Pennsylvania . . . and Jesus stayed behind! There was the awful sense of His absence.

While we are yet young, Jesus goes with us through the most trying circumstances. He stays by our side even when we may be out of the expressed will of God, until one day - that is the drawing line! There is that voice *behind* you. (You have run so far ahead He is talking from *behind* you.)

"Young lady, what is all the running for now?"

Then you begin looking around. Instead of just looking at yourself you say, "Oh, Lord, I am so sorry. Was there something *You* wanted me to do?" *There must come a time in our lives, if we are ever to become mature, when the initiative in our life passes from ourselves to God.*

Immaturity is going where you want to go; maturity is going where God wants you to go. It is that simple!

You say, "I think I will go visit my sister today."

The Lord replies, "Not today. I want you to stay home today and complete those unfinished projects."

"But Lord, I always visit my sister on Tuesdays."

"Yes, I know, but now you go at My bidding and you stay home at My bidding. It is time for discipline. Now the time has come for you to begin to realize that I am your Lord! I am giving the orders." Your Savior is now becoming your Lord!

From Cocoon to Butterfly

The ramifications of commitment to divine guidance, as understood in this book, produce a metamorphosis in the life of the believer. We pass from the bondage of a cocoon to the freedom of a butterfly by the process of death to the old and resurrection to the new. In divine guidance we go from a self-willed and sin-bound person to a new creature enjoying the full liberty of the mind of Christ and the ministry of the Holy Spirit. We have not been reduced to a mechanized robot. *Guidance is not a bypassing of our personality; it is an enhancing of the moral freedom of a disciplined son who has learned to please his Father.*

Stripped of dependence on feelings, desires, and the tyranny of human reasoning, we can walk in obedience. These are the things that have held us captive, and as we die to them, they are returned to us as our servants and not our masters.

Once we were slaves to feelings; now we are free to enjoy our feelings. Once we were slaves to inordinate desires; now our desires flow toward Him who promised that as we delight ourselves in Him, He would grant us the desires of our heart. Once we were bound by the limitations of human understanding; now in the resurrected Christ we are tapping the source of all truth, wisdom, and knowledge.

This is what Jesus meant when He said, "For whoever wishes to save his life shall lose it; but whoever loses his life *for My sake* shall find it" (Matt. 16:25).

This is what Jesus Himself did, and this is what God the Father wants to do. This is how we become conformed to the image of God's Son.

The Fully-Guided Life

Paul wrote to the Galatians, "I have been crucified with Christ; and it is no longer I who live, but Christ lives in me; and the life which I now live in the flesh I live by faith in the Son of God, who loved me, and delivered Himself up for me" (Gal. 2:20). *The ultimate in divine guidance is when the Lord takes the initiative and begins to move you toward His goal for your life.*

The passing of that initiative is your prerogative. God will not wrest it from you. You choose. "I give up the right to take the initiative in my own life, Lord. Here it is. Lead me." You daily confess, "My Father, Thou art the friend of my youth" (Jer. 3:4).

King David perfectly described the fully-guided life:

The Lord is my shepherd, I shall not want.
He makes me lie down in green pastures;
He leads me beside quiet waters.
He restores my soul;
He guides me in the paths of righteousness for
His name's sake.
Even though I walk through the valley of the
shadow of death, I fear no evil; for Thou art
with me; Thy rod and Thy staff, they comfort
me.
Thou dost prepare a table before me in the
presence of my enemies;
Thou hast anointed my head with oil; my cup
overflows.
Surely goodness and lovingkindness will follow
me all the days of my life, and I will dwell in
the house of the Lord forever.

Psalm 23

ABOUT BOB MUMFORD

After receiving a Bachelor of Science degree from Valley Forge Christian College, Bob Mumford attended the University of Delaware, and then received his Master of Divinity degree from Reformed Episcopal Seminary in Philadelphia. He has since served as pastor, Dean and Professor of New Testament and Missions at Elim Bible Institutes and as a popular international conference speaker.

As an author, Bob has written for major Christian periodicals in the United States and abroad. He has published twelve books including, *The King and You, Fifteen Steps Out,* and *In the Face of Temptation.*

Bob is an international conference speaker and Bible teacher with a unique and powerful gift of imparting the Word of God with authority and clarity. He speaks out of more than 35 years of experience and prophetic insight. Countless thousands have attributed their spiritual growth and determination to serve the Lord to Bob's ability to help them understand the ways of God and His Kingdom. He seeks to promote personal spiritual change and growth in the life of every believer without undue reference to denominational distinctions.

Bob resides in Raleigh, North Carolina with his wife, Judith where they are surrounded by two of their four children and several grandchildren.

Also Available by Bob Mumford

Lifechangers Tape, a monthly teaching tape where Bob, in his humorous and direct style, deals with pertinent issues that effect our everyday lives. Some past titles have been:

- ❖ Church of My Dreams
- ❖ Running on Empty
- ❖ Model of Friendship

Plumbline, is a monthly booklet which handles relevant subjects about the Christian life. Some of the past issues have been:

- ❖ Forever Change
- ❖ Standing in the Whirlwind
- ❖ Barriers to Intimacy

A catalog of other materials by Bob Mumford is also available. Contact Lifechangers at P.O. Box 98088, Raleigh, NC 27624 or call (800) 521-5676.

Reach us Online

You can also order materials and get current information through our Website at: **www.lifechangers.org**.

We'd appreciate hearing from you!